MY

ONE

AND

ONLY

MY

ONE

AND

ONLY

The Special Experience
of the Only Child

―――

ELLIE McGRATH

―――

WILLIAM MORROW AND COMPANY, INC.
NEW YORK

Library of Congress Cataloging-in-Publication Data

McGrath, Ellie.
    My one and only : the special experience of the only child / Ellie McGrath.
        p.   cm.
    Bibliography: p.
    Includes index.
    ISBN 0-688-06488-4
    1. Only child—Psychology. 2. Only child—Case studies.
  I. Title.
HQ777.3.M35   1989
155.4'42—dc19   88-37064
                                      CIP

Printed in the United States of America

First Edition

1 2 3 4 5 6 7 8 9 10

BOOK DESIGN BY BARBARA MARKS

For Julie Holloran McGrath

CONTENTS

INTRODUCTION

I was sitting in my office one morning, alternately gazing at the Hudson River and perusing *The New York Times,* when the phone rang. An acquaintance, a woman I knew from running in Central Park, had a question for me. She had her first child when she was in her late thirties, and she was now forty. "I understand you're an only child," she said. "I'm torn about whether I should have a second child or not. I'm not sure it's fair. How did you feel about growing up an only child?"

Fair. What an interesting concept, I thought. As anyone over the age of ten knows, life is certainly not fair. Nor had it ever occurred to me that there was anything inherently fair or unfair about being an only child. I had never considered the possibility that someone would have a second child just because she did not want to be guilty of making her first-born an only child.

What I didn't realize at the time was that this woman was quite remarkable. Most people come from families of two or more children and grow up assuming that anything less than a foursome is not really a family. This woman at least was willing to explore the issue of what it means to be an only child.

So I struggled to answer her questions as objectively as possible. I had never really drawn up a balance sheet, analyzing how I felt about being an only child. My mother had died, after a long battle with cancer, when I was six. That loss had so shaped my life and psyche that I had never focused much on what it meant to be an only child.

In looking for pros and cons, I could come up with advantages more easily than disadvantages. I had been well cared for and well loved. I had enjoyed being the center of attention, at least most of the time. I had always felt endowed with everything I needed. I was grateful that my family had put sizable resources into sending me to an excellent private college, where I was able to bloom.

Was I lonely? That was perhaps an obvious question. And indeed, sometimes I had missed the company of a peer. Occasionally, I could have used an ally to even the odds in those intermittent skirmishes with adults. But I had lived in a neighborhood where there were several other children in my age group. I sometimes felt I had the best of both worlds: friends by day, sanctuary by night. As I got older, I chose friends whom I believed would be with me for life, several of them only children themselves. So I didn't feel lonely, except in that deep, aching way that everyone must feel at some time or another when things could be better.

Nonetheless, I felt a great responsibility in offering this

woman advice. I didn't want to persuade her to stop at one child, even though that was what I thought she should do. My experience, I felt, was not typical, so I should try to give her the most even balance sheet I could conjure. To bolster the debit side, I mentioned that friends had thought it was a disadvantage to be an only child with older parents. And I observed that an only child could have a heavy burden as parents became ill or infirm.

The next time I saw this woman she was pregnant.

I decided to write this book because I wanted to find out the truth about only children. Just because I had had a reasonably happy life didn't mean that there weren't thousands of only children, huddling by a lonely fire, desperate for the sound of a human voice. Since I had spent most of my career as a writer for *Time* magazine, I set about doing the research as any journalist would.

I began to read articles and research that had been done on only children. We were, I discovered, a controversial subject. The positive articles protested too much, trying to assure parents that one child provided them with the best of both worlds, a parenting experience coupled with fewer burdens. The negative ones reiterated the old stereotypes about only children being lonely, selfish, and maladjusted. As I started to do my own research and talk to people, I was astonished by the amount of prejudice against only children. I asked one friend if she knew of any articulate only children who would be good to interview. Her reply: "Oh, you should talk to Susan, she's the perfect only child—self-centered, introverted, driven." Great, I thought. This is what my *friends* think.

I found out what many of the psychologists, educators, and social scientists had discovered about only children through questionnaires, observations, and controlled studies. Then I set about identifying some interesting only children. I was fascinated to find some famous people who had virtually nothing in common except their single status: William Randolph Hearst, Jean-Paul Sartre, Frank Sinatra, the Duchess of Windsor, Leonardo da Vinci, and Indira Ghandi, to name a few. I thought that only children were pretty rare, until I started noticing that the subjects of many obituaries in *The New York Times*—Mary Astor, Cary Grant, Roy Cohn, for example—were only children. But compelling as these people were, I needed to talk to the living.

I was most interested in hearing the stories that only children, themselves, had to tell. I considered an individual an only child if he or she had grown up without brothers or sisters—although a few of the people interviewed had a step- or half-sibling. The latter individuals qualified as only children because there was a substantial age difference (ten years or more) or little contact with step-siblings.

I interviewed well over a hundred only children, many of them through tape-recorded interviews and others through more casual conversation. Some only children were referred by friends and professional researchers; some responded to advertisements. The sample was not scientific, but it was representative. I spoke to only children of all ages, from six to seventy. The majority were college-educated (as most only children are), but there also were dropouts and seekers. Their eagerness and honesty made me realize how important it was to set the record straight.

Many factors shape a life: family traditions, childhood experiences, education, good books, close friends, career, marriage, opportunities seized, opportunities lost, and, of course, good luck. The importance of siblings varies from individual to individual; the absence of siblings does not. As

I talked to only children, I found that being the only one is a definitive fact of life.

One of the most important questions, I found, was to ask *why* a person had remained an only child. Few other people ever ponder family size. How many oldest children, for instance, ask their parents why they went on to have another child or two? (Wasn't I enough? You wanted a boy, too? Such conversations seldom take place.) But only children, so often confronted by the stereotypes of strangers, must grope to justify their single status.

As I listened to individuals explain why they thought they had been the only child, I realized that I was actually quite typical. I was an only child because my parents married old and my mother died young. Other people often brought up late marriages and fertility problems. Those born during the Great Depression reflected on how one child was a perfectly normal choice, given the economics of the times. Many of us were only children because of historical traumas or non-conformist parents.

All of that, of course, is beginning to change. There are many good reasons why the one-child family is becoming a more popular choice today. The development of safe and reliable birth control has allowed women and their partners to plan the timing and number of children. Some experts estimate that it costs $150,000 to raise a child today—even before college—making large families increasingly rare. In addition, many women who have invested in education and careers are not willing or able to relinquish their jobs and professions for full-time domesticity. Many organizations demand that a man or woman put the job before family, friends, and personal interests in order to succeed. Flex time, shared jobs, and part-time work, still rarely available, are generally accompanied by lower pay, status, and potential for advancement. While many women have told me that they can manage that delicate balancing act of working and parenting with one child, a second child can tip the equilibrium.

Social scientists indicate that the facts about only children are more positive than the fictions. A number of studies have found that only children do better in school, form good friendships, and tend to be high achievers. Even the intangibles seem to be positive. The great majority of only children I interviewed were very satisfied with their lives. So were parents of the lone child.

But there is no question that people's feelings change over time. Now in my mid-thirties, I am very happy to be an only child. I believe that some of the traits I most value in myself—independence and imagination, for instance—are directly attributable to growing up as an only child. I don't long for a sibling, in part because I believe my close friendships are better than many sibling relationships. Because two of my closest friends are also only children, I feel confident that those bonds are as lasting as family ties.

Yet, as I was in the middle of writing this book, I happened to be looking through some old college papers. I found an essay entitled, quite unoriginally, "Autobiographical Sketch." Evidently, a teacher had asked us to write about ourselves. I had no recollection of ever having addressed the subject of being an only child. Yet here in front of me was a very negative little essay. In it I wrote: "I was always told how lucky I was to be taken along to all vacations, anniversary dinners, and family weddings, times when youngsters were usually dumped with baby-sitters. Unfortunately, by the time I was a teenager, I was so tired of adult company that I wanted to be abandoned to my own schemes the way kids whose 'parents didn't care about them' were." I went on to write about how much I enjoyed being part of a dormitory, even though I sometimes missed my privacy. Yet looking back from fifteen years later, I can recall how traumatic it was for me to have to share a room with another person and how lucky I was that my roommate was another only child. I also remember my great relief at finally having a room of my own my junior year.

The point is that recollections can shift like dunes in a nor'easter. We see events from different perspectives as time passes. In the following chapters, you will read many anecdotes told to me by only children. I have counted on the accuracy of memory, a risky reliance. Talk-show host and author Dick Cavett, an only child whom I interviewed for this book, summed up the problem. "It was not until my first book came out," he said, "that I realized that an entire story I told was false in the sense that the other party in it was someone other than the person I had remembered. I also talked about my grandfather in a certain way, and then I got to be friends with one of his sons, my uncle, whom I had hardly known until the last few years of his life. He had a totally different impression of the old man. I had to think: Could I have been so wrong?"

In the course of more than one hundred interviews, certain themes came up again and again. They reflect the views of those individuals at a particular stage of their lives, to be sure. But they also form a distinct pattern, one that seems to approach truth. There is no single "authorized" version of what it's like to be an only child, just many interpretations.

Being an only child is not perfect. There are some disadvantages, as in any of life's situations. But there are also wonderful things about being the only one. Just as I was unwilling to urge my acquaintance to stop at one child, my aim in this book is not one of advocacy. I would simply like to challenge the assumptions many people make about only children. This book is an attempt to reveal some truths that are not necessarily self-evident—and to explore the special experience of the only child.

THE

MYTHOLOGY

*T*he picture was taken by a Kodak Brownie camera, one of those square black boxes with a crystal viewfinder. No one under the age of twenty-five could possibly remember them. I am in the center of the picture, wearing a winter coat and leggings, even though there's no snow on the ground. My father is standing on the top step with me, and my mother, who's the tallest of us all, is a step below.

The year is 1956. We are posing in front of our new home, a blue ranch-style house in Gloucester, Massachusetts. There is still a plank where a walkway should be. But otherwise, the house looks ready. It's fully painted. The knocker is on the door. There are even curtains hanging at the window. We look like we're the beginning of the American dream.

My parents are a bit old, by fifties' standards, to have a four-year-old. My mother is thirty-five and my father, forty-seven. And much as my parents might have wished for Father Knows Best domesticity, we are *not destined to be a "normal" American family. My mother has been diagnosed with cancer. The odds are not very good. So my grandfather, an architect, has rushed the contractors to finish this house so that my mother can get some enjoyment out of it. Ranch-style houses are very popular, but my grandfather designed this house on one floor because he knows that if my mother lives, she will be an invalid.*

She did not live, although she would not die for another two years. But our family would never grow: I would be the only child. And I would feel different. As I made friends at kindergarten and went off to school, I would discover that everyone else had a mother. Everyone else had a brother or sister.

Only children may be victims of one of the last unexamined prejudices in this country. It is not the kind of prejudice that denies you a job or excludes you from clubs. It is much more subtle. When it comes to kids, double or nothing has been the American way of life. At least publicly, Americans have had many a romantic notion about children. A "real" family has always meant two or more tykes. Norman Rockwell's visions of happy families have outlived the *Saturday Evening Post. Leave It to Beaver,* the popular television series with mom, dad, and two sons, may be a relic of the fifties. But the eighties equivalent, *The Cosby Show,* features even more Huxtables. In advertising, the family of four is still used to sell everything from hot dogs to hardware.

Just as the family of four is considered "normal," our culture mandates the only child to be, at best, different; at worst, abnormal. Only children are supposed to be lonely, maladjusted, unhappy, and selfish. They are believed to be the spoiled brats who throw fits if they can't get their own way. Or the Superchild who can do trigonometry before he can drive a car. Or the shrinking violet who's tied to Mama's (or Daddy's) apron strings.

Ruth Ainslie, a New York lawyer and mother of two, thought she was totally out of step as an only child growing up during the Baby Boom. "I always felt it wasn't a family, in the real, American sense," she recalls. "I thought the balance was wrong: two adults and one child. I always wanted a sister and brother. I really felt that we were being un-American."

It is astonishing to me how much American culture has changed, even in my relatively short life span. I have seen the civil rights movement bring minorities a greater degree of justice. I watched in school as NASA put a man on the moon and cried nearly twenty years later when the Challenger blew up. I've benefited personally from all the new options that the feminist movement opened up for women. I've been entertained by the *Star Wars* of George Lucas and scared by the star-war technology of Ronald Reagan. Attitudes have changed about so many things: love and war, sex and marriage, race and gender. But one idea seems to remain the same: The ideal American family size is two children.

Gallup Polls, those popular barometers of public opinion, point out the extent of the resistance to one-child families. About 78 percent of Americans believe that only children are disadvantaged. It was true in 1950, and it remains true in the 1980s. In 1973, only 1 percent of the population said that they considered one child to be ideal. In 1986, that figure had risen to only 5 percent. By contrast, 59 percent of Americans believe the two-child family to be ideal.

There is a prejudice, deeply embedded in the American psyche, that needs exorcism. Roberta Graham, a writer living in Alaska, tries to articulate it, as she ponders why she feels compelled to have a second child. "When I was growing up, I had one brother and two sisters," she says. "Down the street from us, there was a family that had just one child, and my mother always acted like this was a sad family, that they weren't normal. Now I have one child, and in many ways I'd be content to keep Katie as an only child. But having siblings is almost like being raised Catholic. There are some ideas you can't shake."

The psychological community may actually have created the notion of the disadvantaged only child. The eminent G. Stanley Hall, who trained many of the first American psychologists after the turn of the century, once declared: "Being an only child is a disease in itself. . . . Because of the undue attention he demands and usually receives, we commonly find the only child selfish, egotistical, dependent, aggressive, domineering, or quarrelsome." One of Hall's contemporaries, A. A. Brill, concurred: "It would be best for the individual and the race that there should be no only children."

This is pretty strong stuff. Yet even back in the 1920s, when psychologists actually studied only children, they found them to compare very favorably to children who had brothers and sisters. Two studies published in 1927, for instance, found only children to be more intelligent and more verbally adept than those with siblings. Another 1920s study indicated that only children had fewer behavioral problems in school.

Today, there is a wealth of data. Originally, researchers turned to only children as a way to compare the impact of siblings on a child's development. But in the 1970s, social scientists and psychologists began focusing directly on only children. Toni Falbo, an educational psychology professor at the University of Texas at Austin, and Denise Polit, director of Humanalysis, Inc. in Saratoga Springs, New York, surveyed five hundred studies that have included only children. Their conclusion: "The popular and negative views about only children are not valid. Only-borns were not found to be at a significant disadvantage relative to their siblinged peers."

Yet prejudices persist. Judith Blake, a demographer at the University of California at Los Angeles, in reviewing surveys taken on family growth, found that the majority of Americans believe it is a serious handicap to be an only child. She found that over half believe that only children have some sort of personality problem, such as being self-centered, spoiled, or anxious. About a quarter believe the only child is lonely. Blake points out the irony: "Only two percent of respondents believed, even when asked directly, that the major disadvantage suffered by only children is prejudice from teachers, neighbors, relatives, or other children."

Disapproval of others can be communicated to only children early on. In a study of one- and two-child families, psychologists Phyllis A. Katz and Sally L. Boswell of the Institute for Research on Social Problems in Boulder, Colorado, discovered that children tend to consider onlies "lonelier, bossed by friends, spoiled, and socially maladjusted." They noted: "It is clear that eight- and nine-year-old children are very much aware of the stereotypes associated with only children and believe them."

Indeed, as I talked to only children from all over the country, I kept hearing the same refrain: We want to set the record straight. "I don't think of myself as spoiled," says Christine McManus, a student at Tulane University. "I don't like that myth at all. It's a myth propounded by people who have siblings." Ann Fisher, an advertising executive who lives in the San Francisco area, enjoyed being an only child, but admits that she was affected by stereotypes. "I was one of the only only children I knew growing up in the 1950s," she says. "I felt different. There was an assumption that you were spoiled. I felt like I was constantly bucking some of those images."

I, myself, can remember the inadvertent unkindness of

others. A child would occasionally walk up to me and ask, "Are you spoiled?" And I used to think, "Why do you ask? Have I done something wrong?" I'm convinced now that other children were parroting their parents. Or cuing in to messages they were receiving from books and television. Remember: Dennis the Menace was an only child.

Many children's classics reflect the cultural stereotypes of only children. One of my favorite books as a child was *The Secret Garden,* written by Frances Hodgson Burnett. I was drawn, I think, to the mystery, not to the message so obvious to me now. In *The Secret Garden,* Mary Lennox, a recently orphaned only child, comes to live with her uncle at the mysterious Misselthwaite Manor. At first, she is nasty and demanding, a classic spoiled brat. But eventually she discovers her sickly cousin Colin, also an only child, self-exiled in a hidden part of the house. Colin, the ultimate spoiled brat, informs her: "Everyone is obliged to please me." Mary, of course, rebukes him, causing Colin's long-suffering nurse to concede: "It's the best thing that could happen to the sickly pampered thing to have someone to stand up to him that's as spoiled as himself." The moral: By becoming more like siblings, Mary and Colin shed their cloaks of selfishness and redeem themselves.

The heroine of Kay Thompson's 1955 classic, *Eloise: A Book for Precocious Grown-Ups,* is the outrageous only child of juvenile literature. Rich and pseudosophisticated, Eloise is the quintessential hellion, the prankster queen. She lives at the Plaza Hotel, and her every whim is room service's command. Her mother is always away and her nanny is always tired, tired, tired. So Eloise spends her time playing tricks on adults and outraging their sensibilities. Her audacity is endearing, but she is also willful and obnoxious. Eloise, while amusing, is very hard to take.

Of course, the image of the spoiled only child is conveyed not just by fiction. I was curious to see what Dr. Benjamin Spock, the Moses of mothers, would have to say about only children. In various editions of *Baby and Child Care,* which has sold over thirty million copies, the subject of the only child has been addressed chiefly in relation to spoiling. In his introduction to the 1976 revision, Spock, who happens to be the first-born in a family of six children, writes: "The main reason for this third revision of *Baby and Child Care* is to eliminate the sexist biases of the sort that help to create and perpetuate discrimination against girls and women." That is a salutary endeavor. However, even today, in the fortieth anniversary edition, spoiling and only children remain inexorably linked in the index like Siamese twins.

Another pediatrician, Murray Kappelman, wrote a book called *Raising the Only Child.* While Kappelman, an only child himself, draws from personal as well as professional experience, the whole premise of the book seems to be that only children have special problems (true) and are not really like other children (false). For instance, in a chapter entitled "The Onliness of the Only Child," Kappelman writes: "Evening often finds the only child facing a companionless world . . . The young only child's heightened irritability during the hours before bedtime often expresses both a sense of absence of peer companionship and an attempt to force increased parent-child intimacy as a replacement." Not an encouraging picture.

The American media, too, are often unenlightened about only children. Positive research findings seldom make their way into the popular press. When they do, the "good news" stories seem to protest too much. "Only Isn't Lonely (or Spoiled or Selfish)" proclaims a 1981 *Psychology Today* story. "Sometimes It's Good to be an Only Child," says a 1986 *Parade* magazine headline—implying that many other times it's not so hot to be the only one. For every positive article about only children, there are dozens of pronatalist pitches. Despite the present low fertility—or perhaps because of it—there has been a barrage of information on how to push the upper limits of childbearing or how to adopt a baby.

Much of the bias against only children is unstated. But every once in a while, a writer makes an overt attack. I was taken aback to see an article printed in the *Chicago Sun-Times* in 1986 that bugled: "Only-child syndrome is a threat to American society." The author, Bryce J. Christensen, an editor at the conservative Rockford Institute, writes: "It is in the give and take between brothers and sisters that most people first learn a sense of cooperation and of shared community." Christensen goes on to condemn people who "choose yuppie comforts over a second child" and to charge that the upbringing of only children leaves them ill-prepared to be the parents of more than one child. The trend toward one-child families, he fears, will leave an aging society without the necessary support. Christensen concludes: "Will a half-size generation made up of only children shoulder these burdens or will they be too absorbed in their own private problems? If the one-child family is truly 'the wave of the future,' perhaps we'd better brace ourselves for damage along society's shorelines."

Christensen reviles a Lilliputian generation of only children in part, perhaps, because of unstated religious beliefs ("Go forth and multiply"). But he also opposes only children and low fertility for economic reasons. Anyone who reads the newspapers knows that once the Baby Boomers retire, there may not be enough workers to support the Social Security system. Ben J. Wattenberg, a senior fellow at the American Enterprise Institute and author of *The Birth Dearth,* believes that there are global implications to the present U.S. birthrate of 1.74 births per woman, the lowest in history. Wattenberg maintains that the baby bust will bring about serious economic problems and, eventually, the decline of Western influence and power.

The only child's image problem transcends cultures, however. I've been quite interested to note the rash of bad publicity in American newspapers and magazines about the one-child policy in China. A headline for a 1982 *New York Times* article, written by Christopher Wren, declares: "One Side Effect of Birth Control in China: The Brat." The article explains that China's population, already estimated at over one billion, must go no higher than 1.2 billion people by the year 2000. The country's ability to feed itself and survive may depend upon the one-child family. Yet, the first paragraph of the article says: "China's drive to hold down its population by restricting couples to one child has created an unintended side effect—the spoiled brat."

Toni Falbo has done extensive research on only children both in this country and China, where she has served as one of eleven foreign experts at the Child Development Center of China in Beijing. "The Chinese do have similar thoughts about the only child," explains Falbo, "but it's somewhat different. Some of the traits only children have, like autonomy, we would think is good. But in China, they see that as bad. Only children violate the traditional values in China more than they do here. The concern that I hear now among teachers and officials is that only children want to do what they want to do. Or that they're weepier. That they're not as self-controlled. In the U.S., egocentrism is regarded as something fairly good. We would see a lot of this as pretty normal behavior."

Part of the problem in China, of course, is that the government has forced the one-child family on many Chinese. In

some cities, there are birth quotas. Marriage is frowned upon
for women under twenty-four years old. A woman who
wants to have a baby must fill out an official permission
form in order to get pregnant. If she will sign a one-child
contract, she will be given an extra three months of paid
maternity leave. If a family has more than one child, the
parents lose their "model worker" status. To try to enforce
the one-child family, old women, called the Granny Police,
visit a woman's home to make sure that she is taking her
birth-control precautions.

The government policy violates powerful traditions. Post-
ers may proclaim: "Have Fewer Children but Raise the
Quality" or "A Single Child Is Cause to Be Proud." But they
are no match for the ancient Chinese blessing: "May you
have a hundred sons and a thousand grandsons." Since the
son and his wife take care of his parents, having a daughter
as an only child can be a catastrophe. The result: a rise in
infanticide in China.

Interestingly enough, in the spring of 1988, the U.S.
granted political asylum to three Chinese couples who said
they feared persecution because they had violated China's
one-child policy. Thousands of people from around the
world are denied entry into the U.S. every year, despite
political and economic hardship. Yet in 1988, the Reagan
Justice Department adopted new guidelines requiring immi-
gration officials to give special consideration to Chinese who
object to their nation's one-child policy.

However, in some Western European countries, particularly West Germany, the one-child family has become
widely accepted. West German women have an average of
1.3 children; that is, at least half the families have one child
and less than half have two. "Until recently, American
women were more likely to go to school, get married, and
have children," says Esther Mechler, a member of the board

of Zero Population Growth, who has studied fertility in West Germany. "German women married later and were on their own longer. Even after they married, they waited longer to have children. There were space considerations, too. A lot more people in Germany live in apartments. Here it's more normal to have a house. In Germany childbearing is a more thoughtful process, whereas Americans tend to rush out and do it."

American fertility patterns have changed dramatically with the times. In colonial days, the young nation had one of the highest fertility rates in the world. When the birth rate was measured for the first time in 1820, as the frontier was being settled, women averaged seven or eight births, with five children usually surviving. American fertility began declining at the turn of the century as the U.S. evolved from an agrarian society toward an urban nation. Women who were born in 1908 and would begin starting families in the late 1920s had an average of 2.2 children, and more than 20 percent had no children at all. Then during the Depression, many couples married later or decided that they could afford only one child. As a result, there were many only children who grew up during the Depression.

As World War II began, fertility rates began to rise again. In 1942, total births topped three million for the first time. As the war ended, the multi-child family became the ideal for Americans of nearly every social class or ethnic group. Even social service agencies would not allow a couple to adopt just one child because a lone child was considered a hazard to himself and the family. Then came the Baby Boom. Between 1946 and 1964, about seventy-six million babies were born. There were many social factors at work: post-war euphoria, a recessionary economy, and high material expectations. What's more, Rosie the Riveter, who had taken a man's job during the war, had to be encouraged to do something else. As a result, women marched into suburbia, where they were rewarded for producing babies. In that climate, one child was not an achievement, it was an embarrassment.

Given the fact that only children were common and accepted during the Depression, it seems obvious that the Baby Boom exacerbated latent prejudice against only children. "For most of my childhood, I was an anomaly," says Laura Stein-Stapleford, thirty-five, who runs her own public relations business in Williamsburg, Virginia. "I went to a Catholic grade school, came from a good Catholic family, but had a last name that didn't sound Catholic. A comment that I'll never forget was made to me in the fourth grade by a bus driver. She said, 'Your parents must not be very good Catholics if you're the only child.' " In fact, Laura's mother had unsuccessfully tried to have more children.

Some of the selfishness projected onto the only child was perhaps an assumption of the selfishness of the mother. An only child had once been the result of some misfortune, physical or economic. After the advent of effective contraception, one could look at a woman and assume that she decided to stop at one child. "In the fifties, having an only child became something that could be chosen," says Mary Catherine Bateson, the only child of anthropologists Margaret Mead and Gregory Bateson. "And it was a selfish choice, made by nasty, egotistical women, probably career women, or women who didn't want to spend time or money on children." Margaret Mead, who suffered several miscarriages before giving birth to Bateson, always publicly emphasized her desire to have children. Says her daughter, looking back: "Margaret was saying, 'I'm not one of those selfish women who chose not to have children.' "

Bateson, herself an anthropologist, argues that the nuclear family of the fifties was a very dangerous place for an only child. "The woman had no other real life outside the home," she says. "She was alone with a baby and vacuum cleaner all day long in the suburbs. It was rather severe isolation that was a pressure cooker for Oedipal triangles. The only protection for children from that emotional focus was that there be several of them."

Although some of the prejudice against only children is irrational, there are two powerful reasons why people have been reluctant to have only one child. One obvious reason is that many couples want the experience of raising both a boy and a girl—as the song goes, "a boy for you, a girl for me." Indeed, statistics show that people will tend to have three children if two girls or two boys are born first.

The other major reason why people want more than one child is that if an only child dies, there are no other children. Given the emotional investment parents make creating a family life, losing an only child can be devastating.

However, the death of any child is a tragedy, whether an only child or one of six. Adam Clymer, an editor at *The New York Times,* lost his only child, Jane emily, who was killed by a drunken driver just as she was beginning her junior year in college. Clymer, himself an only child, talked about Jane emily's death over a year later. "From what I know from parents who have dealt with this, it isn't any easier for parents who have several children," says Clymer. "The only conceivable way in which it may be simpler for them is that it gives them one more argument for trying to function normally: You can't go to pieces because there are three other children who need you. I don't think that what happened to us is harder to bear. I think if we had been younger, we might have tried to have another child. But this sort of thing doesn't happen that much. Not many kids die before their parents."

Despite all the perceived drawbacks to being an only child or having an only child, a surprisingly large number of people actually are only children. According to the Population Reference Bureau at the Center for Health Statistics, there are about eighteen to twenty million only children living in the U.S. today. During the Depression, one out of every four or five children grew up without siblings. That number dropped to about one in ten during the Baby Boom.

Who are only children? Three sociologists at Ohio's Bowling Green State University, H. Theodore Groat, Jerry W. Wicks, and Arthur G. Neal, put together a profile of the adult only child, using a sample of twenty thousand married men and women from the National Survey of Family Growth. Of all married adults, 6.1 percent of husbands and 5.8 percent of wives were only children, supporting the theory that parents are more likely to stop at one if a boy comes first. The researchers found that only children are more likely to be Protestants than Catholics, given the latter group's ban on birth control. Only children are also more likely to be of Jewish or European ancestry and to live in urban areas of the Northeast. In computing the proportions of all women who have ever been married and given birth, the researchers found that 16.5 percent of white and 17.3 percent of black women have been mothers of one child.

Today, only children are once again on the rise. Fertility has reached an all-time low, as women exercise career options, aided by reliable contraception. Today, the average number of children in American households is 1.85. The Bureau of the Census found that the number of married women expecting to have one child has risen to 11 percent from 7 percent in 1960. However, the numbers of only children exceed those expectations: As of 1978, 17.9 percent of married women between the ages of thirty and thirty-four had only one child, as opposed to the 11 percent who actually intended to have just one. This statistic, which reveals a difference between intention and reality, indicates that the new popularity of one-child families may actually be the result of delays in marriage and childbearing, rather than active choice.

"Everything points in the direction of an increase in the proportion of only children," says Charles Westoff, Director of the Population Research Office at Princeton University. "There will be a decrease in the number of children as there is a delay in childbearing. Since the first child will occur at a much later age than has been the case historically, the probability of having a second child will diminish for all kinds of reasons. One is that women will have satisfied the urge to be a mother without having a second child. Another is that costs of all kinds will increase with a second child."

As the number of only children increases, will their image improve? It's too early to tell. Sharryl Hawke, an educator who has studied only children and has mothered one child herself, observes: "I don't think people have changed their minds about the mythology. I think the conditions of present-day society have made it more attractive to think about only children."

A TALE
Susan Shwartz, late thirties, science fiction writer, New York City:

Being an only child is definitely one of the things that shaped my life. In fact, I'm afraid it's pretty much at the core of it. My parents married

late, and my mother could have only one child.
She was thirty-seven or thirty-eight, very old in
those days.

I remember being a little girl and being a Blue-
bird. When the other kids were brats, that was
cool. If I was a brat, which I was likely to be, too,
other mothers, women younger than my mother,
would say 'spoiled only child brat!' Now perhaps
the problem was an economic one. My father was
a lawyer and better off than the husbands of these
women. My family was Jewish. None of these
people were. All I could think of was that I was
somehow marked as a spoiled only child brat,
which is a hell of a lot of disapproval to bear when
you're six or seven years old. It makes you feel a
little freaky.

However, within my family when I was a kid,
things felt fine. I had been very concerned that
there were no male Shwartzes of my generation,
and I asked my father if this bothered him. The
name would not go on. He said, no, that he knew
it was likely that Mother would have one child,
and he had been praying for a girl. Wasn't that
great! Eldest daughters or only daughters are frequently reared as if they were sons, but I was
reared as the much-wanted and much-awaited
daughter. This was wonderful.

Nevertheless, as an only child, I was sort of like
an only doll in some ways. It wasn't that I had
power over them, but I had to be perfect, like Lady
Jane Grey. I was the sole, precious egg in the bas-
ket, and I couldn't screw up. The clothes had to be
right, the hair, the face, the manners. I still cannot

yell when I'm angry. I think I was good as a little doll. I don't think I was too good as a person.

Then when I was a teenager, I realized two different things. The first happened when I was walking our neighbor's two Norwegian elkhounds, two big dogs. I saw how they got along, how they were always nipping, skirmishing, and playing. And then a third elkhound came in, and it was an only elkhound. Though it was bigger than the others, it was getting the shit beat out of it by the others because it did not know how to pretend-fight. And I realized that I didn't know how to pretend-fight. I had three modes: freeze, run, or go for the jugular. And the skirmishing that brothers and sisters would do would terrify me. Because I knew that if I went into that yell-mode, I was going to fight to the death.

Then when I was fifteen, I realized that I was able to fight back. We had high school sororities, and there was going to be a party. My parents went out and got me a nice costume. At the same time, we gave a ride to the party to another girl who lived on the same street. Both her parents were working hard at a delicatessen to establish themselves. So we drove the girl to their delicatessen so that she could be approved by her mother. Her mother approved her, then looked at me and said, "Is that new?" I said yes. She said, "It must be nice to be an only child." I looked at her and said: "You know, people have more charity to bastards than they do to only children. I can't help it, either. And I don't like it." This is an older woman, and I'm under ferocious discipline to be deferential to adults. I'm in her store, my father is standing there. He didn't say anything. It was okay for me to deal with this. Thereafter, I realized that anyone who said anything to me about only children was going to get hurt.

I found that being an only child was a good thing, in terms of closeness with my parents, although it was rough if they were both mad at me. As an only child, I shared a great deal of things with my parents. I know my love of science fiction, which I'm now writing professionally, comes from my father. In terms of ability to interact with adults, being an only child was wonderful. If I wanted peers, I had to earn them, which meant that I had to develop social skills and I had to be able to share. I didn't have any kids who had to play with me because I was their sibling. So, in some ways, being an only child was very, very good.

Still, it was a cruelty to a young girl to get this amount of grief from what I now realize were envious parents. Zero Population Growth came along as an utter godsend, because I could say that my parents were more socially committed than anyone else's. I'm thirty-seven years old now. When someone says "only child brat" even now, I call them on it.

two

THE

TIE

THAT

BINDS

*E*very once in a while, I take a look at my baby book. It is bound in pink satin with a little bow on the front. I open it up and the first thing I see is a card taped to the inside cover that begins: "God bless you in sleeping. God bless you in waking, God bless you at eve, And when grey dawn is breaking." The tape has yellowed, but the card has never slipped from its place.

Next comes the formal birth announcement, and another card. It reads: "Announcing the arrival home of Eleanor Burns McGrath, otherwise known as Torie (short for Tornado)." Legend has it that I was born during one of the few tornadoes ever to strike Massachusetts. The name Torie, thank God, never stuck. The next page says that I was named Eleanor, for "light," after my grandmother. My mother notes that at my baptism, I "didn't cry once, a perfect little lady." There is a page for weight ("7 lb. 9 oz. at birth"), and even for teeth. My mother notes: "Just three

months old! Her first tooth arrived the day Eisenhower was elected President." I guess that really dates me. I come to a family page that is
imprinted with a little homily: "A family where there's more than
one / Is really nice and much more fun."

The entries stop after eleven months and don't begin again until I'm
five. When they resume, they are written with a different hand. My
mother is still alive, but I have gone to live with her sister, my Aunt
Mary, and my Uncle Jerry. They are in their forties and have no
children. So for a few years, I become the only child of four people.

My aunt and uncle lavished attention on me. They had always wanted
a child and had been unable to have one. My uncle was a pied piper, who
loved children and would have liked to have had four or five of his own.
He and I were great companions, spending hours together gardening or
going to the beach. My friends were always welcome at our home, and
he often was the leader of the games. He'd play tag and hide-and-go-seek
with as much zeal as the rest of us. I felt lucky to have my aunt and uncle,
and eventually I realized that they, too, were lucky to have me.

After my mother died, when I was six, I usually saw my father once
or twice during the week. My maternal grandparents lived virtually
across the street from him, so I could combine visits. I think he was lonely,
living alone. On the weekends, my father and I would take excursions,
sometimes to Boston to see a movie or into Ravenswood Park for a walk
in the forest. He used to spar with me, and we'd argue for an afternoon.
He later told me he did this so that I would know how to stick up for
myself.

Throughout my childhood, my mother lived on, at least in spirit. To
the others, she was a dear woman who had left them too soon. To me,
she was more of an idea and an ideal. I conjured her image from others'
descriptions. She was witty and popular, slender and handsome. She had
graduated valedictorian of her college class. She had been a brilliant
teacher. All her students loved her. But more than anything else, I was
told, she had wanted to be a mother. She had wanted to be my mother.

The highest compliment that anyone could give me was, "You're just *like your mother." I wore my hair the way she would have liked me to wear it, in curls. I could be sitting in the living room, reading a book, and hear whispering. I'd look up, and my aunt would say, "Oh, you spoiled it. For a second, the way you were holding your head, you looked exactly like your mother." After her death, I was told that everything of hers was mine: her clothes, her books, her diamond rings, even her teaching materials. As I got older, I would dress up in some of her fancy evening clothes and pretend I was she. I declared that I would become a junior high school teacher, just as she had.*

I felt closely connected to my four parents. It was hard not to. Three of them were always there, watching me, caring for me. The fourth was in heaven, literally looking over me. My mother did continue to live. I made sure of it. I was her legacy.

In some ways, childhood is a fantasy world inhabited largely by adults. A parent tries hard to give his or her offspring an ideal life, a perfect childhood. Yet, a child accepts virtually any reality. Gloria Vanderbilt, an only child who was the focus of a notorious custody battle, put it best in her autobiography: "In the beginning a child believes that all other children are in the same world that she or he inhabits. That is how a poor child defines all others, and that is how a rich child defines all others. Once upon a time it never occurred to me that my situation was in any way singular or different from that of every other child in the world."

The relationship between parent and child is probably the most fundamental in life. There may be no other bond so complex. It can be a fierce and passionate attachment. It can be distant and full of unrealistic expectations. But a child, at least for a while, is totally dependent and accepting. As I interviewed only children, I was struck by how closely their youthful happiness corresponded with how well their parents had handled their sense of disappointment—or their feelings of joy—over having had just one child.

What kind of people have just one child? In their 1977 study of only children and their parents, Sharryl Hawke and David Knox found that about 40 percent of mothers and 23 percent of the fathers had grown up in large families of five or more. About 10 percent of the mothers and 18 percent of the fathers were only children themselves. While the average American woman has her first child at twenty-two, most of the mothers of only children are much older, often in their thirties when they have their first and only baby. Hawke and Knox found that while not all the single-child families were planned—some were the result of divorce or uncontrollable circumstances—the parents reported a high level of satisfaction with their families. They cited financial advantages, more time to enjoy their child, a closer relationship, and less stress on marriage and career. Yet, over half of the parents in the study had been criticized for stopping at one child by relatives, friends, and neighbors.

I found that there are four major categories of only children. There are the unintentional only children. Their parents may have envisioned enough children to start a baseball team, then found that economic or fertility problems defeated them. Or they may simply have married late or waited too long. If those parents convey their frustration, the only child may feel inadequate. On the other hand, such an only child may feel cherished and secure. It all depends on the parents' reaction. "I had wanted more children and was told it would not be safe for me," says Bella Bankoff, an apartment superintendent in New York City. "I had the one child. I never thought of it as being an advantage or in terms of being less work or less costly. I was just very glad to have one child. When Lisa came along, I was thankful for a great favor. In my case, maybe it was better to have only one. My husband was a traveling salesman, and the whole job of raising her right through her teens was mine."

Some children, such as myself, remain the only one because of a death in the family. They obviously have different problems than those children who had parents who tried and failed to give them a brother or sister. The problems, though, are often related more to loss and separation than to growing up alone.

Many children remain without siblings because of their parents' divorce. More than a third of marriages end in divorce today, and only children are overrepresented in broken homes. Those children may be the flotsam of a shipwrecked marriage or the prize of a custody battle. According to the U.S. Census Bureau, there are more single mothers with just one child than with two. About 20 percent of all single parents are bringing up one child. Jill Schwin, a personnel manager in her late thirties, had her first and only child at eighteen. "My first husband really pushed for a while to have another one," she says. "And I just didn't want to. He felt at the time that the marriage was falling apart and that having another child would be a way to keep us together. I knew better. I knew I was going to end up leaving, and I would have two little children instead of one. I knew one was going to be difficult enough on my own without having another."

Finally, there are the only children by their parents' choice. They tend to be very positive about their lives and feel that being an only child is as natural as having brothers and sisters. People have a variety of reasons for choosing to have one child. They can range from financial problems to career aspirations to a desire to remain more independent. Sometimes, too, the birth of a first is so difficult that a parent fears another ordeal. Patricia Dalzell of Massachusetts stopped at one, even though she was still in her twenties, because her baby, Pammy, went into fetal distress. "The whole thing was a real trauma to me," says Dalzell, now forty. "I was very frightened. It was a few years after that when I decided I just couldn't do it over again. I was just very happy to have her, and as time went on, it just seemed that it was not necessary to have another child."

In *Up Against the Clock: Career Women Speak on the Choice to Have Children,* authors Marilyn Fabe and Norma Wikler explore the benefits and problems of combining child raising with a career. The authors note: "We've repeatedly heard women say that with one child they could manage to keep up with a career, but with a second, everything came apart at the seams." It is a theme I hear echoed by my contemporaries, capable women who care about their professions and their families, women who are dubbed "superwomen" by the media and eventually interviewed for their insights on burn-out.

I began to notice in my readings that many famous women were the mothers of one child. Somehow, it is not surprising to find actresses, who are notorious for unstable marriages and a preoccupation with youth, mothering few children. Liv Ullmann, Lindsay Wagner, Susan Sarandon, Tammy Grimes, Ann Sothern, Bette Midler, and Gwen Verdon, to name a few, have given birth to just one child. Just the same, when a book called *Starring Mothers* was published in 1987, I was surprised to see that twenty-one of the "thirty accomplished women" chosen by the authors were the mothers of one child. They were not all actresses, either. Designers Donna Karan and Betsey Johnson, Astronaut Dr. Anna Fisher, Businesswoman Georgette Klinger, and Writer Erica Jong were all mothers of one. Although some of the thirty women were young enough to have more children, most were past their childbearing years.

As I began to pay more attention to the family patterns of people in public life, I discovered lots of one-child families. Soviet leader Mikhail Gorbachev and his wife, Raisa, are the parents of one child. Jimmy Swaggart, the now-disgraced evangelist preacher, and his wife, Frances, said that they had stopped at one child because they felt guilty that their traveling had forced their son, Donnie, to go to thirty-one public schools around the country. When Arkansas Governor Bill Clinton announced that he would not run for President in 1988, he cited the strains it would put on his family: his wife and their only child.

Alice Walker, who wrote *The Color Purple,* talked eloquently about choosing to have one child in a speech she gave at Sarah Lawrence College a decade ago. Walker had resisted having "children" because she was afraid that they would destroy her ability to do serious work. "My first mistake was in thinking 'children' instead of 'child,'" she said, recalling how her own mother had struggled with eight sons and daughters. After Walker had her baby, Rebecca, she felt that she was changed forever. Birth, she said, might be "the one genuine miracle in life." So then why have only one? "Because with one you can move," she said. "With more than one you're a sitting duck."

Parents of one child often have been depicted as people who really don't like children and have been reluctant to make a commitment to family life. My sense, though, is that the opposite may be true. These parents, despite the fact that they may be busy professionals (or perhaps because of it), often have dynamic relationships with their only child. Dianne Feinstein, the former mayor of San Francisco, says that she wanted to have more children, but was unable to do so. She worked from the time her daughter, Katherine, was in nursery school, and she was involved in politics by the time her daughter was in elementary school. Feinstein, who was the eldest of three children, believes that a mother must provide the same level of care whether she has one child or three. Feinstein admits, though, that there were a lot of advantages for her in having only Katherine. "If I had had a number of children, it would have been much more difficult to have become active when I did," says Feinstein. "Having one enabled me to do more things."

Katherine, now thirty, remembers: "I always used to get mad at my mother. When I was a little kid, my mother was the only one who was both divorced and who worked. And I was the only only child. I used to get really furious. She would never drive the car pools. She would never go to the PTA meetings. She fed me a lot of frozen food. It used to make me crazy because she was so different."

Today, the two describe their relationship as very close. "I think in a lot of ways there are a lot of likenesses between the two of us," says the former mayor. "Now that Katherine's married and she's working as a deputy D.A., it manifests itself really in the sense of friendship and to a great extent, camaraderie." Katherine observes: "I have a relationship with my mother that is different from everyone's relationship with their mothers. My mother and I both have the most incredible ability to make the other one completely crazy. There is camaraderie, too. It has to do absolutely with my mother's job. I think people have really been intimidated by her presence. They want to please her, they want to say the right thing. I have none of that. To me, she is my mother; she's always been my mother. So we're very direct. We have a lot of mutual respect. We can also make each other laugh in ways that other people can't."

*   *   *

Most only children can go through life confident of one fundamental fact: They were wanted. According to the Office of Population Research at Princeton University, 15 percent of all children who are born today are actually not wanted. However, researchers Sharryl Hawke and David Knox found that the one-child family is generally carefully planned. The researchers observe: "In contrast to larger families in which babies often come along at unscheduled and inconvenient intervals, a single child in a family is usually the result of specific intention and careful timing by parents."

That planning and anticipation tends to make the only child the object of undivided affection. "I have loved being an only child," says Elizabeth Clark, a woman in her mid-twenties living in Irving, Texas. "I'm real, real close with both my mother and daddy. My mother said that she just wanted one, and that if I hadn't been a girl, she would have left me at the hospital. She had been an only child, and really liked being an only one. I think when people only have one, they've really thought about it."

One high school English teacher who grew up in rural New York state, echoes Clark. "I think the most important thing for me as an only child was really knowing that I was wanted and loved and cared about immensely," she says. "I knew I was the focus of the family, and there was so much love coming toward me that it compensated for any other problems. I tried to satisfy my parents by excelling in a great number of activities, from the school play to sports to academics. I don't think they really cared at all about any of that. They were just really happy with this kid they had."

A sportswriter friend of mine recalled how moved he was the night Roger Staubach was awarded the 1963 Heisman

Trophy. As a quarterback on the football team at the United States Naval Academy at Annapolis, Staubach had become a phenomenon, appearing on the covers of both *Time* and *Sports Illustrated.* When his father was asked to say a few words at the Heisman dinner, he rose and said: "God gave us only one child, but He gave us a good one."

Looking back now, Roger Staubach says he had "a great relationship" with his parents. "I had a quality at an early age, whether it was fighting a bully on the playground or whatever," he says. "I just never quit. When I was in a tackle-football game on the sandlot, I just came back fighting. When I was most discouraged, I seemed to try harder. I don't know what that was. Part of it was the fact that I always wanted to please my parents. I loved them a whole lot. I wanted to do well for them. I also knew that to do well, you always have to work at it. I just wanted to pay the price a little more than other kids."

Interestingly enough, when I asked people to name the greatest advantage and disadvantage of being an only child, many of them came up with the same answer: their close relationships with their parents. In many respects, the intimacy is positive because it sustains, provides security, and makes the only child feel important. At the same time, it can rob an only child of privacy and inhibit independence. But many of the only children I talked to believe that the closeness is natural and nurturing.

Early on, only children realize that they have a fairly exclusive relationship. When I talked to six-year-old Frederick Bouchardy, a first-grader in New York City about how he felt about his family, he admitted that there are times he'd like to have a sibling, but he also knew that a sibling could detract from him. "I would hate it if my parents had a baby and had a party and no one paid attention to me and my parents," said Frederick. "If they only paid attention to the little baby, I'd be invisible. I'd be the invisible one."

A well-balanced trio can be as nimble as the three musketeers. Ann Fisher, an only child in San Francisco, recalls: "We three were extremely close. We called ourselves a circle, a threesome. Sometimes I'd get jealous if they left me out. I felt I was better friends with my parents than most children are. I was treated as an equal as well as a child."

A strong sense of security can accompany an only child throughout life. Ruth Brine, a retired magazine editor living in New York City, had a close, almost sisterly, relationship with her mother. "One reason Mother didn't have more children was because she wanted to be an opera singer," says Brine. "Even after I was born, she and her mother went to New York for six or eight weeks. She didn't get anywhere, but she still worked on her music. When she'd go away to Chicago for piano and singing lessons, we'd think of each other at the same minute. We always had a time of day, say six o'clock, when we'd think of each other. My father was a doctor and didn't take much part in family life. My mother got up early in the morning with me from the time I was three and practiced piano with me. For years I would practice an hour on the piano, an hour on the violin, until I went away to college. You don't get up and do that unless somebody really cares. I gave up music for many, many years, but I'm grateful to her because music is very important to me now."

Bill Brennan, a television and theatrical producer in his mid-sixties, says that he misses his parents very much. Even though he has five children and eleven grandchildren, it is the relationship with his parents about which he seems to feel the most tenderness. "My dad was my closest friend," he explains. "He was never an authority figure; he was my friend. My problem was that I was devoted to both of them. I've often thought over the years: Thank God my dad was the strong kind of guy he was. He was a bright man and he was for me. When bad things would happen, we would walk down the street arm in arm. We'd kiss full on the lips. We stayed close. When I was flying a lot in the fifties and sixties between New York and L.A., I'd fly into Omaha and some-times I'd just have a day. They'd meet me and we'd take a hotel in Omaha or drive home to Waterloo. We grabbed all the extra times we could together."

Brennan particularly remembers the time he was working at CBS in New York and his father, who was then president of the Western Iowa Bar Association, asked him to speak to the group about television. "It was a big day," remembers Brennan. "The men played golf and the women played bridge. Then I was the featured speaker at the big dinner that night. After playing golf, we were in the locker room and the guys were pouring the drinks, saying, 'Come on, Bill. What do you want?' Dad says, 'No, Bill, don't have anything.' He was very concerned about my speech. I had brought a co-axial cable, which was the device they origi-nally used to put the network together before they had microwaves and all that. When I went to go get it from the trunk of the car, Dad said he'd go with me. We got the stuff out, and he said, 'If you do a good job, I'll give you a hundred dollars.' It was so like him. He so wanted me to do a good job. It wouldn't have mattered if he said ten cents—I knew how much it meant to him that I did a good job."

The only time Brennan's closeness to his parents proved to be a problem was when he went away to college in Cali-fornia. "It was too far away," he recalls. "Remember, this was 1938. Distances were a lot greater than they are now.

My parents were having some problems, so my father told my mother: 'He can't go unless you go.' It was a convenience for him. There were a lot of family friends who said you're going to cramp his style. She asked me, 'Well, do you think I will?' That put a guilt thing on me if I said yes or no. So my mother came to California with me. Compared to a lot of people, it was great. I had a nice place. I was well-clothed and well-fed. But I missed that typical college experience. So I resented that a lot. We didn't have too many bad decisions, but I thought that was a bad decision."

Fiction has cast a fisheye at the intensity in the one-child family. Erich Segal's pop classic, *Love Story,* reflects the common stereotype of the unhealthy closeness between parent and only child. Before Oliver Barrett IV, the charming preppy, meets Jenny Cavilleri's father, he thinks: "Here I would be bucking that lotsa love Italian-Mediterranean syndrome, compounded by the fact that Jenny was an only child, compounded by the fact that she had no mother, which meant abnormally close ties to her father." And Oliver was right. After he shakes Phil Cavilleri's hand, Jenny and her father lock in an embrace: "For a split second nothing happened. And then they were hugging. Tight. Very tight. Rocking to and fro . . . I was definitely odd man out."

The issue, of course, is whether only children and their parents have destructively close ties. And, again, the answer depends on the family. There are legendary examples of too-close relationships between a parent and an only child. Elvis Presley, the "King," was an only child after his twin died at birth. The rebel of rock 'n' roll lived with his mother, Gladys, well into adulthood, until she died. One biographer wrote: "From Elvis's first moments on earth until his mother's death some twenty-three years later, Gladys Presley never stopped worrying about his every waking moment. . . . She was intuitive about her child, and several people who knew her in those days and in years to come would call her 'psychic' about Elvis." After she died, Elvis never discussed his mother with anyone but his father and refused ever again to watch his second film, *Loving You*, because Gladys appears in the audience.

Roy Cohn, the notorious lawyer who aided the McCarthy witch-hunts and eventually died of AIDS, would seem to have little in common with Elvis. But he, too, was an only child who had unusually close ties to his mother. As a young man, Cohn would admit that he was a "mama's boy." Indeed, as biographer Nicholas Von Hoffman points out, Cohn and his mother, Dora, "lived together until she died, forty-two of Roy's fifty-nine years."

Actress Brooke Shields, another only child, might be called a mother's obsession. For over a decade, magazines have chronicled how Mother/Svengali Terri Shields has pushed her pretty baby into modeling and movies. Even after graduating from Princeton, a time when most young adults seize control of their lives, Brooke Shields seemingly still defers to mom.

For most only children, the intensity is more subtle. When two people are adults and the third is a child, the dynamics can be difficult, the balance of power, lopsided. Carmelita Thomson, a psychological therapist who lives in Eugene, Oregon, was born in Oklahoma during the Depression to a woman who was eighteen. Because her mother was so young, Thomson feels that they were like sisters. At the same time, though, Thomson found that her closeness to her mother also robbed her of privacy. "It was impossible to have a secret life," she recalls. "She always knew what I was doing. I think there tends to be a boundary problem. And because there aren't any other children, a parent doesn't have to respect that boundary. It's a very contradictory thing, because, on the other hand, my parents were relating to each other, and I was left out."

Some only children find the focus of attention almost overwhelming. One woman now in her early thirties was born to parents who were thirty-seven and thirty. They had earlier given birth to a child with Down's Syndrome, who had died when he was a year old. "I think it took all the courage they could muster to try again," she says. "Once they got me, they took real good care of me. They practically kept me to themselves. I did play with other children. It wasn't bad, but it just seems there was an awful lot of the three of us. I was brought up under a magnifying glass. Everything I did that was good was much, much better and much more worthwhile than it really was. And everything I did that was bad was much worse and exaggerated out of proportion."

It's no fun to be a majority of one, especially when you are a child. Sherri Elliott, a sales representative living in California, believes that an only child can get short shrift. "Instead of having more attention paid to you," she says, "it's just the opposite. The two adults spend time with each other and the kid doesn't get anything. You kind of tag along or are worked into whatever they want to do. Take something like Disneyland, for instance. If you have a family of three kids, the parents may say, 'Let's take the kids to Disneyland.' When parents have one child, they don't plan a vacation for the kids. You have to do what they're doing. I think it's easy for the parents to lose sight of the age of the kid and what's important in a kid's life."

If there is an unusual problem with a parent, one child may be forced to tolerate it, while the presence of more children might hasten its solution. One man in his forties, who is a professor of English, had a rough time growing up because of his mother's obsessive cleanliness. He recalls: "The house was run according to very strict rules that had to do with all aspects of life, large and small. These rules included taking off your shoes before coming into the house, putting your clothes in a specific place. Nobody, including my father, could even touch the refrigerator. And I mean TOUCH the refrigerator. I don't, even when I go back now. It's just off limits. I never got a drink of water for myself because this was her domain. There were all these rituals having to do with cleanliness that, I'm sure, would be very interesting clinically to someone. But my mother would never get help because people of that generation just didn't. I had to live this way, and I think my being an only child was a factor, since it was two to one. I really was victimized by that. I don't think my mother would have been able to maintain her routine if there had been two or three children. It would have cracked the limit of her endurance. I would have had a confederate of my own, instead of being sort of co-opted by my father as his ally."

The professor believes that his family's problems were exacerbated by the fact that his parents were forty and forty-five when he was born. Although it is fairly common today for men and women in their forties to have a first child, it was quite remarkable in the 1940s, especially in a working-class neighborhood in Denver. "My parents were old enough to be my grandparents," says the professor. "When I was ten years old, I was really becoming aware of this. I would realize the parents of my friends were thirty-two, while my parents were well into their early fifties by then. I was always, I'm ashamed to say, embarrassed by them at hot dog roasts for Cub Scouts. There were all these other dads who were running around playing touch football with the kids, and my father was not quite up to doing that. The final irony, of course, is that both of my parents have outlived everybody else. They're now in their eighties and in perfect health."

As baby boomers delay marriage and childbearing, older parents are becoming increasingly common. Currently, about 150,000 babies a year are being born to first-time mothers aged thirty to forty-four. Many of these babies will be only children. In her book, *Last-Chance Children,* Monica Morris, a sociologist at California State University, Los Angeles, explores the problems of having older parents. She interviewed twenty-two people who were born when their parents were anywhere between thirty-five and fifty-two. While many of the twenty-two had positive things to say about the opportunities and attention they were given, there were a number of common complaints: feeling different, worrying about parents' mortality, dealing with a generation gap. In a chapter devoted to only children of older parents, Morris finds that these only children can become isolated, especially during their teen years, if their parents are too old to have empathy for their concerns.

In his memoir, *Half the Way Home,* Adam Hochschild, the founder of the liberal monthly magazine *Mother Jones,* describes the chilly relationship he had with his father, a wealthy and conservative capitalist, who was nearing fifty when his only child was born. "There was always a stiffness in the air between us, as if we were both guests at a party and the host had gone off somewhere before introducing us," writes Hochschild. Yet his mother, who was forty-two when he was born, was his constant companion, comfortable in a child's world. Hochschild continues: "My greatest fear of all in those years, which I never dared voice to anyone, was that she would die and I would be left alone with Father."

It is wrong to assume that only children of older parents are automatically handicapped. Chances are older parents are stable, both financially and emotionally. While older parents may not have the energy they might have had ten or twenty years earlier, they may have more time to spend with a child. Betty Ann Byerly, a data processor who lives in Greensboro, North Carolina says she had a great childhood. Her father was forty-two when she was born; her mother, thirty. "I think because my parents were older, my mom and I spent a lot of time together," Byerly recalls. "On a rainy day, we'd walk around the house and sing. She taught me to whistle. I was into being a cowboy at the time. I'd come downstairs in the morning, and she'd say 'good morning' like I was some sheriff. I'd say 'Good morning, ma'am.' She'd put some Coke in a shot glass and say, 'You want the regular?' It was great. I even asked for a football helmet for Christmas one year, and they gave it to me."

Older parents may appreciate children more than young adults who are still exploring the world themselves. Helen L. Mamarchev, thirty-seven, who is associate vice-president for student affairs at the University of Florida, thought that being the only child of older parents was a great advantage. "They probably were comfortable with themselves and had worked out a lot of things," she says. "They allowed me— encouraged me—to be independent. I didn't think there were limits to things I could do."

Yet, there is one potentially devastating problem with older parents: They sometimes die when their children are still relatively young. Mamarchev's father died when she was fifteen. "It is somewhat bad to have children late in life," she concedes. "I'm just now beginning to appreciate my mother. She was a wonderful role model. I wish I lived closer to her. She's at the end of her life, and our time together will be cut short."

Not only do single children tend to have older parents, an estimated 35 percent of them have parents who are divorced. Many people assume that divorce is harder for an only child to cope with than it is for children who have brothers and sisters, with whom, presumably, they can share their family's troubles. Divorce puts an incredible amount of stress on any child, but it is not clear whether it is any harder if the child must go it alone.

Some important evidence indicates that only children fare a little bit better than children with siblings when a family splits up. In 1980, Denise Polit, director of Humanalysis, Inc., a non-profit research organization, interviewed 110 families within three years of a divorce so that she could specifically compare only children with other children whose families had gone through a divorce. The average age of the mothers was between thirty-two and thirty-five, and the children were typically ten or twelve.

Polit found that only children in single-parent families seemed to adjust better to the divorce than children with siblings. Only children appeared better able to keep friends, both juvenile and adult, during this time of stress. In addition, they appeared to be more independent, showed high self-esteem, and were described as more mature and empathetic by their parents than children with siblings.

Since female-headed households are among the poorest in the country, it stands to reason that in such households, one child will be easier to support than two or three. Yet the reason an only child is better off goes beyond the obvious division of resources. Polit found that single mothers with two or three children were often forced to live on welfare, while the mothers of one child were more likely to be able to work full-time. Women with one child were able to adjust more quickly, both psychologically and financially, to life without a mate. As a result, those families became stable sooner.

Very few people who have seen their families divided by divorce have anything good to say about the experience. However, divorce often makes the only child extremely self-sufficient. Harriet Benson, a woman in her forties who works for a California pharmaceutical company, did not find that the advantages of being an only child were canceled out by her parents' divorce. "My mother and father were divorced, and my mother worked," she explains. "I don't recall that that was ever particularly a problem for me. During my grade school and some of my early high school days, I was pretty much on my own. I read a lot. I listened to the radio a good bit. I was never conscious of being lonely. I usually saw my father twice a week, but I can't recall that those were exciting highlights of my life. We did things in the evening, but I don't suppose I had a lot of attention. My mother and I never disputed anything I did, because she just really had to trust me to do everything by myself. And I did."

Some only children, though, feel betrayed by divorce. Sherri Elliott's parents split up when she was in her teens. Although she was "best man" at her father's second marriage, she does not feel a part of the new family unit. "As a child, I was raised very traditionally," she says. "Thanksgiving was always spent with certain people, Christmas was always done a certain way. There is none of that anymore. Everything that I was taught as a child to be sacred and true—what life's about—is no longer valid. It's amazing how fast that can all be pulled out from under you when your family is so limited. All of a sudden you find out that you're independent and alone."

Remarriage can pose a particularly big problem for the

only child, who is not just losing a father or mother but gaining a stepparent. Käthe Roth, a Canadian born in Germany, felt that her parents did her a disservice both by stopping at one child and getting a divorce. Her stepfather, she says, was a very strict disciplinarian. And she admits that she was jealous of him and his relationship with her mother. "There was a fairly constant battle for my mother's attention," she remembers. "My mother told me often in my teen years how torn apart she was feeling because my stepfather and I really waged battles. I was an active person in that triangle."

Perhaps the biggest problem facing an only child in the aftermath of a divorce is how to divide his or her time. Barbara Graham, a playwright, divorced her husband when her son, Clay McLachlan, was two. She has written a play, *Jacob's Ladder,* that dramatizes the strains that quarreling parents can inflict on an only child. In the play, Will, the fictional father, states: "The fact is, the present arrangement stinks. Two parents, one kid. Mom and Dad both want kid. Law of psychology: Kid wants both parents. Law of physics: Kid cannot be in two places at one time."

The drama continues in real life. "I'll never forget Clay's graduation from junior high school," recalls Graham. "He had this incredible retinue: his father and his new stepmother, his mother and his soon-to-be-ex-stepfather, as well as the man who was to become his new stepfather. I felt so sorry for him. Here was this wonderful little kid with all these adults hovering over him." Although Graham was granted primary custody, as Clay began to get older, she allowed him to divide his time between her and his father. "Sometimes I worried that the burden might be too much for him. There were two of us, who had very different values and lived very different lives, and only one of him. I've tried very hard to keep him from feeling divided. So far, it has worked out all right, because Clay has developed some perspective about it. And the bottom line is that both his father and I love him very much and have been there his whole life. That's what matters most."

Clay is aware that his situation is unusual. "I didn't know anything else when I was younger," he says. "I thought people were lucky if they had parents and could live at home with them. I don't know a lot of kids who switch homes. It's hard to change life-styles every week or so." Holidays are especially difficult because he spends the morning with one parent and the evening with the other. "It was sort of weird," he says. "I didn't really like having to deal with four people, but I also didn't want anybody to feel left out." Now seventeen and ready to go to college, he looks forward to getting out on his own. "I didn't choose between my parents," Clay says. "I split it equally. In a way, I took the easy way out. On the other hand, it was harder on me. I don't think it would have been that much easier with siblings." Now that his dad has remarried, Clay has a three-year-old twin brother and sister. He says he likes having the connection. He believes: "They'll be around."

When you are an only child and a parent dies, you face a special burden. David Giveans, an early-childhood educator and publisher of *Nurturing Today* in San Francisco, still feels very close to his mother even though she died over forty years ago when he was just nine years old. "The first nine years of my life were quite extraordinary," says Giveans. "I was the blessed event. The whole family revolved around me. My mother, especially, made me out to be a little god. I went to women's club meetings with my mother and learned to balance a plate of sandwiches and say 'please' and 'thank you,' all of which has stood by me greatly over the years. I had a very secure life."

But Giveans's mother became ill when he was still very young. "I think my mother had a premonition of her death," he says, "because she would take me to the cemetery where she was subsequently buried, and we used to walk among the tombstones. It was like a reading lesson. What does this one say, can you read that one, aren't the flowers pretty? One day she suggested we pick some to take home. Because I had always been taught not to take things unless one asks, I distinctly remember saying to my mother, 'Well, how can we take these flowers; they aren't ours.' And I remember her saying, 'I don't think the people here will mind you enjoying their garden.' So after Mother died, I never went to the cemetery. I went to the garden to visit Mother."

Within a year, Giveans's father remarried a woman who resented the boy. "When my stepmother moved into the house, it was like a window shade was pulled down on this beautiful world I had known. She discouraged me from anything that Mother encouraged. Sometimes she had a terrible temper and would chase me around the house. But the worst thing was going to bed at night as they argued about me. My poor father was between the devil and the deep blue sea. He had promised Mother, on her death bed, that he would always take care of me. And this he did, but at great personal expense. My stepmother never knew that my father helped me pay for college. She would have been furious."

Giveans still struggles with the loss of his mother. In his home, he has a photo album. The inscription reads: "This is a loving record of your life, lovingly accumulated by your Mother, whose whole life was your father and you." Giveans sighs: "I think Mother planted so much creativity and curiosity in me, because she had this premonition of her early death. Had she lived, I think she never would have allowed me to grow up. She would never have allowed me to be the person she created."

A FAMILY TALE
Deborah Carey, early fifties, teacher, Amherst, Massachusetts:

Having one child was not a decision we consciously made. We had been married for ten years before Merritt was born, and we had sort of given up on having a child. I was thirty-two, which really isn't that old by today's standards. When Merritt was born, she was a cesarian they did at the last minute. After the cesarian, there was something that didn't respond right medically for an hour or so. We later talked about whether we would adopt another child, and we decided not to. I think our main concern had been whether Merritt would have been better off with siblings.

I think it's fun having an only child. I think you get to be a lot closer to the child. It does mean you can do more things. The child doesn't control your life, because you can just pick up the child and go somewhere. It's easier with one than with more than one. I continued working after Merritt was born. George was teaching at the University of Maryland and had mornings free. He would take care of her three mornings a week, and two mornings we would have this wonderful woman who was of the old school. She had been a foreign service wife, but was now about eighty. She would bring Merritt little Mexican chairs. She'd say, "Merritt needs to learn to eat in the restaurant," and she would drag her to Howard Johnson's.

When we moved to Amherst, Merritt was two. I decided it would be better for me to work full-time than not at all. I'd go bananas not working at all. And I knew I couldn't get a part-time teaching job, because they're very hard to get. So, Merritt was in day-care. I noticed that after a couple of weeks Merritt was crying all the time. And she was normally a pretty cheerful kid. So I said to myself, there's something going on here that isn't quite right. I realized I was getting home from school at three-thirty or four o'clock with a pile of schoolwork which I would do. She'd always been used to a lot of time with her parents. So I said to myself: Well, I'm not going to bring school work home. And I never have. What I sacrificed was long talks with my colleagues. To me that was worth it. It was the first time I had to make a decision, and once I made that decision, it wasn't hard to stick to it.

When Merritt came to seventh and eighth grade at the junior high school, which is where I teach, I didn't know how that would be for her. But she would come running in in front of a classful of kids and give me a big hug. It was surprising because kids at that age tend to reject their parents.

She talks to me a lot more than I talked to my mother about relationships. We've talked about things like birth control. I can't imagine her discussing her male relationships with George at any length. But she would with me. I tend to take it very seriously, which it is for the person at the time. If she asks my advice, I will tell it to her. Usually she's pretty sound about things anyway. I was surprised because I never talked to my mother about anything.

We were in Albany in June because Merritt had a crew race. While we were waiting for the race, one girl started to tell a story. Then she said to me something to the effect that you can't tell mothers a lot of things. And Merritt said, "Not me; my mother is really cool." That was neat, in front of all her peers.

She talks to George about different things than she talks to me about—values relative to herself or about being alone. This year she went through a hard time when she and a friend were trying to separate. She would come in with tears and then go out on her own and establish herself as a separate person. She wrote George a letter, not about it in relation to him, but in relation to finding strength in herself. So it's that kind of self-reliant thing that she talks to him about: understanding why he likes to be alone.

Basically my position with Merritt is that I'll do anything for her that I can do. I don't think it's done her any harm. I think the choices she makes are usually very good ones, and I don't see any point in interfering with that. And to the extent that I'm capable of supporting her, there's no reason not to. She has a lot of self-discipline, which I think she learned from her competitive riding. I think this idea that you have to deprive them to build their character is garbage.

George Carey, mid-fifties, folklorist, Amherst, Massachusetts:

The biggest advantage of having one child, quite frankly, has been practical. Why not? It allows us not to worry about education. Obviously, she is going to get the best of what we can give her. And she's going to get it without having to borrow, beg, or steal. That in itself is a kind of relief, since education is a prime thing for us. It's fulfilling to know she's going to get the best that we can offer. I like it just from the fact of having a real focus with just this one child. But then again, I don't have anything to play it up against. I watch other people with two or three children, and they seem to like that as much. The disadvantage of having one is putting all your energies into spoiling that child. There is a focus there, no question. All your good things, but all your bad things, too.

Deborah and Merritt have a very close relationship. My relationship with her is different. Deborah says: "You're her spiritual counselor, and I'm more her everyday counselor." I don't counsel her but I talk to her about, say, my relationship to my family place in Maine and what it means to me— and what I hope it will come to mean to her. And she writes me letters that talk about that. They're very gratifying. When I was living here in Maine alone, I would sometimes write Merritt a long letter, some fatherly advice instead of writing a journal entry that day. I got a wonderful letter from her, the kind of letter a father wants to get from a daughter. She said: "I now understand why you go down East. You want to be by yourself. I never really wanted to be by myself, but I can see that it's important. I can understand how the loneliness is a positive thing."

I had some fixed ideas about how I wanted to see my child raised. I didn't want to see her growing up the way I had, in a formal and very structured background, which was more a reflection of the era than anything else. Swearing in the home is okay. I've often said that I don't want my daughter to learn to swear from some young punk. I want her to learn from a master. And she has! In my own way, I pushed Merritt to make what I perceived as the right moves. She may react and come around to being a much more formal person. I don't know. Obviously, when you only have one kid, you're going to make her tough. She has certainly never been a feminine woman. I guess she was denigrated by some of her peers who are. But she was feeling sorry for them because they didn't have her confidence.

Deborah and I talked, of course, about having more children at one time. But I guess I was almost scared about having another child. We made it okay with this one. I was always afraid of having a child who was deformed or had something wrong. We talked about adopting a child. I think we were both fairly involved with our professions by that time. Having a second child was not really a high priority. More children with both of us having a career would have been quite difficult. There's no question it can be done, and I think my wife could do it. She's a very energetic woman. But it would just be more of a burden. I never had any regrets I can think of now about having one child. I never wanted a son.

Merritt Carey, late teens, student, Amherst, Massachusetts

I tell my mother everything, everything. Most kids really hide stuff. I've always just told my mom because I figure if I tell her, then she knows and she's not going to get suspicious. I think that is so much better because then she can't think, "God, my kid's away at school and she's addicted to heroin." She creates an environment so that I can tell her. If she was acting like she was going to just totally mutilate me, I'd never tell her anything.

I don't tell my dad everything. But I think I have a really great relationship with my father, and I respect him a great deal. We're close, but not, well, with my mom I think I'm close like with a best friend. I'm still grateful to my father for raising me as a tomboy because I'm physically strong and mentally strong. I feel a lot of that has to do with the fact that he hasn't let me sit around. I'll help him move lumber and not even think about it.

When you're an only child, you discover most things for yourself. And I find a lot of kids started getting into drugs or whatever through their older siblings. When you're an only child, you're never really rushed to grow up. If you go away to school and you feel pressure and you come home, that's your house. You don't have anyone else pressuring you to do anything.

My parents have never put pressure on me grade-wise or anything. They're so supportive of everything I do. So I let my character build its own self. I wasn't cramped into a corner. I think you're much more free and able to do your own thing as an only child. But on the other hand, I think that a lot of it is your parents. If my parents hadn't been the way they were, if they had put pressure on me to wear fancy dresses when I was three, obviously I wouldn't be the same. When I was five, my grandmother always used to buy me these really fancy dresses from Saks Fifth Avenue, and they just sat in my closet.

I think when you're an only child you can develop much more of your own character. My father sure did raise me like a boy. I was tough when I was little. I was like that all up through sixth grade. But when I went to seventh grade, I totally had to get socialized. That's when you start getting interested in boys. It's a hard time. I felt like my character was being changed against my will. I went through a stage when I wanted to be really popular and so I just changed myself to do that. It wasn't me at all. Then I went away to boarding school and got more real.

three

COMING FIRST: PRIVILEGED AND PRECOCIOUS

I am told by my father that the first word I ever uttered was not "Mommy." It was "more." I was toddling along the street with him and he decided it was time to turn around and walk home. Apparently I wanted to keep going and said, "more." Others confirm that "more" was one of my favorite words as a small child, although they can't swear that it was my first. By the time I was in elementary school, I could see that I did, indeed, have more than many other children. I had every childish game from Candy Land to a Coney Island Penny Machine.

I was taken everywhere: vacations, shopping trips, anniversary dinners. I was left in the care of baby-sitters only twice in my life. In fact, I used to beg to be left with a baby-sitter, any baby-sitter. Because I spent so much time with adults, I did everything to become one. I remember being thrilled in the fourth grade when I was told I would have to wear glasses for my nearsightedness. They would make me look older, more dignified, I thought.

Since my mother had been something of a "fashion plate," my aunt was quite willing to bankroll my interest in fine clothes. I never owned a T-shirt or pair of jeans until I went to college. Growing up, my clothes were always the best—Irish woolens, linen, cotton piqué, suede. I had my share of kilts. But in the fifth grade, I was also wearing suits.

My aunt and I would go shopping together and buy similar outfits. We'd shop in the women's departments, not the children's section. I would go to the beauty parlor to have a "permanent" every few months. On Easter Sunday, my aunt and I would wear our look-alike outfits. Since she wore an orchid corsage, I had one too. I looked like a miniature version of her.

Suitably dressed, I acted as if I were an adult. I developed an air of authority. One weekend I went on a skiing vacation with my two cousins. My older cousin Beth, who was in high school, was reciting some chemistry equations. We had covered similar ground that day in my junior high school science class, so I started piping up and correcting her. Her father praised me. But there was silence in the car after that. I realized I'd done something wrong, something that repelled my cousins.

Most of the time, though, I was rewarded for my airs of sophistication. Every Sunday, I went out to dinner with my aunt, uncle, and grandfather. The four of us would sail off in my grandfather's silver Pontiac Tempest to Landolphe's, a restaurant that seemed to be an inner sanctum of adulthood. I remember how dark it was, with sunlight angling in on red leather seats. I seldom saw another child there, nor did I see a children's menu. Sometimes, of course, I would have preferred to be at the beach. But most of the time, I felt privileged to be a part of this world. I was treated as a person of substance by waitresses. If one ever talked down to me, as some people inevitably do to children, I would sit up straighter, give her a hard look, and simply order my food. But people almost always guessed my age as being older than it was. And

I actually felt flattered. I carefully constructed my adult persona the way some kids build model airplanes.

First come, first served. It's true in restaurants, banks, bus stations—and families. There is probably not an only child alive who does not recognize the privilege of being the first, the last, the only one. Social scientists have long maintained that birth order in the family can be one of the definitive facts of life. The firstborn, for instance, often turns out to be the pathfinder, a born leader. The youngest typically is the indulged baby of the family. A middle child must often work harder to get attention and build bridges between his siblings.

Being born first gives a person a great many advantages. Back in the days of primogeniture, the advantages were tangible: The firstborn son inherited the family land and title. Even today, the first child is nearly always special. Parents have never experienced having a child before, so everything is new and exciting. The firstborn has his parents' undivided attention—and sometimes inherits a hidden agenda. Joan Starker, an urban studies specialist in Portland, Oregon, speaks for many parents of only children when she says, "You have one shot at parenthood, so it's really important." Many parents I talked to were preoccupied about "doing it right."

"A single child gets more early individual attention," says Molly Colgan, a real estate agent in her early forties, who has a young daughter, Belinda. "You have the time to work with her more." Colgan's husband has three grown children from a previous marriage. "I wanted to have a child very badly, and if we were younger, I'd want more than two children," admits Molly. "But you can do a lot with one child: You can have two careers, you can go places. With one, you can put her on your back and go where you want. I've been able to do things with her, like go ice skating, that if I had another baby, I wouldn't be able to do with her. I'd be stuck. It would be years. I'd miss an integral part of her maturation."

Colgan is determined that Belinda gets as many advantages as possible. "Private schooling is very expensive," she says. "It's five thousand dollars even for kindergarten. And that's not all. It's two hundred dollars for dance, two hundred more for her Suzuki lessons to learn to read music and play instruments. It's a very expensive proposition, unless you want your child to go to public schools and have maybe one activity." The Colgans recently moved from Brooklyn to Connecticut, a change that Molly feels will benefit them all, especially Belinda.

As I talked to parents of only children, I got a sense that they might put the child first more than adults who have two or three children. Patricia Dalzell thinks that she probably would not have been able to have the same degree of closeness with her daughter, Pammy, if there had been another child. "Financially, it's much easier to have one," she says. "I didn't have to go back to work. I still don't have to, but I did choose to go back to work last year. I had eight years with her. Actually, finances don't enter into it too much. We'd do fine just on Paul's salary. I'm working now because I want to plan for her education, and I want the best for her. So in a sense, I'm working for her."

There are many ways that parents can sacrifice for a child, and some have nothing to do with money. Annie Edwards, a documentary filmmaker, had her only child, Shauna, when she was still a teenager. Since she bypassed college and soon became a single mother, life has not been smooth for her or

Shauna. "In the first grade, my child was really unhappy in the school she ended up in," says Edwards. "Kids were having knife fights. So I moved, and then we moved again. We moved a lot to get her into a happy school situation. Because I didn't own a home—I sold my home when she was three—I always felt a good school was a priority. I didn't need to live anywhere in particular, but she needed to be in a good school. She needed continuity with the kids in her neighborhood. I always felt she needed to be happy in that time she wasn't with me."

Edwards has strained to provide Shauna with everything she thinks her daughter needs. "I indulge Shauna in every single possible way," she says. "I overcompensated because I felt sorry for her. We've never had a lot of money, so it hasn't been a material kind of thing. It's a really subtle thing, and I think you'll find this true of a lot of single parents of single children: It's hard to say no. It's hard to refuse them anything, even within an emotional dynamic."

Only children are portable. They go everywhere and do everything. Dr. Elizabeth Whelan, executive director of the American Council on Science and Health and author of a book called *A Baby? . . . Maybe,* was at first ambivalent about having a child. Now that she is the mother of a ten-year-old daughter, the ambivalence "seems like a couple of lifetimes ago," says Whelan. "We take our daughter with us wherever we go. We wouldn't dream of going on a vacation without her, because we have so little time with her." When Whelan was invited to present a testimonial speech for the surgeon general, Dr. C. Everett Koop, her daughter accompanied her from New York to Washington. "I took my daughter out of school a couple hours early and a couple of hours the next day. But she met Senator Orrin Hatch, and the surgeon general kissed her. That's something you wouldn't do in a

larger family." Dr. Whelan can think of no disadvantages to
having an only child, at least from the parents' perspective.
"I think there are advantages and disadvantages in being an
only child from a child's point of view," she admits. "My
mother's always saying that we never let our child be a child.
She's always an adult, always a part of our life."

As Annie Edwards points out, only children tend to be
indulged. The indulgences can take many forms: presents,
attention, support, opportunities. Nearly every only child I
talked to, even the unenthusiastic ones, admitted that they
felt they had some clear-cut advantages in being an only
child. Almost every only child is aware of getting more
presents under the Christmas tree than their friends with
siblings. Many go on adult vacations before their peers even
get to Girl Scout camp. Furthermore, most only children
know that if they just show the inclination, they will get
every educational advantage, from private tutoring to
Princeton. Yet despite the bounty, the sense of privilege is
based not so much on money, really, as on the security of
knowing their parents will do whatever they can to help
them reach their potential. Dean Watson, the father of 1988
Olympic bronze medal pairs skater Jill Watson, told me that
he never would have been able to fund the expensive training for his daughter if she had not been an only child. "But
we made the ultimate sacrifice," he says. "Jill and her mother
went to Lake Placid for five years and Costa Mesa [Califor-
nia] for two. My wife and daughter were away from home
for seven years."

This knowledge that their parents are "for" them often
results in a healthy sense of entitlement that has nothing to
do with allowances or inheritance. Baron Bates, the vice-
president of public relations for the Chrysler Corporation,

says he was treated like "bonnie Prince Charlie" when he was a boy. His father left his mother when Bates was seven years old, and he and his mother never really had very much money. "My mother came from a well-educated and not well-to-do family, and acted as if she were well-to-do," Bates laughs. "She never had a good sense of money. But she treated me as if I had an inalienable right to certain privileges. Now, she might have done that if she had had more than one child. But the attitude was: You are the heir apparent; you should go to Exeter and you should go to Princeton. I went to summer camp every year, and none of the other kids in my little town of Boonton went to summer camp. None of this caused me any problems. In a way, I felt I had it coming."

Hans Christian Andersen, the Danish author of such favorite fairy tales as "The Ugly Duckling" and "The Little Match Girl" is a perfect example of an only child, who despite poverty, felt as if he were blessed. Andersen's father was a shoemaker who could not always provide enough food for his family. But he made toys and a little theatre for his son, read to him every night, and urged him to study. Young Hans Christian's poetry eventually won him a patron in King Frederick VI. In 1833, at the age of twenty-seven, Hans Christian Andersen wrote: "It seems to me that life itself is a wonderful poetic tale. I feel that an invisible and loving hand directs the whole of it; that it was not blind chance which helped me on my way, but that an invisible and fatherly heart has beat for me."

Whatever their socioeconomic status, many only children feel good fortune as they grow up, knowing that their parents will support them and sacrifice for them. Even though her father died when she was young, Marjorie Irwin, a retired teacher in Michigan, felt that she had all sorts of advantages, primarily because she was the only child. "You hear so much these days about how awful the one-parent family is," she says. "I think, gee whillickers, I grew up in a one-parent family and didn't think anything about it. I mean, I was sorry I didn't have a father, that I don't have many memories of him, but we certainly got along all right. I had advantages. I think I had every kind of lesson there was: dramatic arts, music, dance. Mother just enjoyed having me do those things, and I just went along with it. I had a very happy childhood."

Being included in activities can make a child feel privileged. Betty Ann Byerly, the data processor from Greensboro, North Carolina, recalls: "When I was growing up, they included me in every vacation. I saw a huge part of the U.S. They were so generous that way. Some kids never got to go anywhere. But my parents included me in a lot of things. I remember the time we flew out to Colorado and went camping. They provided me with rich opportunities."

The material advantages are almost trivial compared to the attention focused on only children. Firstborns and only children have been lumped together in many studies on behavior and achievement. But even in the early part of this century, psychiatrist Alfred Adler found that there was at least one important difference between them: When a second child comes along, the firstborn loses his position of privilege. An only child, however, is never dethroned.

Once a sibling arrives, trouble begins. Psychologists who have observed mother-child relationships in the home have found that the bond with the firstborn deteriorates when a second child is born within a year or so, because the mother focuses her attention on the new baby who needs her more. The mother plays with her firstborn less often, talks less, and says "no" more often. The result: more sleeping, feeding, and toilet problems.

Candice Feiring and Michael Lewis, of the Institute for the Study of Child Development at Rutgers Medical School in New Jersey, conducted a longitudinal study of the differences between only children and firstborns early in life. They found that the firstborn children who acquire a sibling by the age of two show a greater dependency toward their mothers than only children and have a tendency to cry more when they are separated from them. On the plus side, though, firstborns are more likely to develop social skills by themselves, while onlies are more likely to get help from mother.

Life, then, is quite different for the only child than it is for the firstborn. The firstborn gets upstaged. The only child holds center stage for the rest of his or her life. Yet, attention is not always neutral. Used properly, it can give a child a sense of confidence; misused, it can undermine confidence. There is a fine line between overprotection and nurturance. A lot depends on how parents apply the attention; much depends on how the child accepts it.

Margo Howard, the only child of advice columnist Ann Landers, writes in her biography of her mother, *Eppie,* that "something about single-offspring status invites a weird combination of watchfulness and adoration." She recalls that for her fourth birthday party, she was taken to a show at a nightclub. "For better or worse," she writes, "I was one of those kids said to be six going on eighteen." The irony, though, was that Margo was never allowed to have a bike or to take the bus to school. "Mother was protective and to some extent fearful, so my activities were restricted," she writes.

Joan Steiger, who became a lawyer after her only son went

to college, admits that she made a few mistakes at first. "Your only child remains your first child forever," she says. "And all the anxiety you put into that, when you overdo parenting, just comes to rest on the shoulders of that one little child. I realized at one point that I just was becoming too intense, and Jeff started stuttering. He stuttered for a week or two. My husband and I had been planning to go away for a weekend. We hired a very nice motherly lady to take care of Jeff over the weekend, and when we came back, he wasn't stuttering anymore. I was thrilled. I knew enough to lighten up so it wouldn't come back. I went through the same thing on thumb-sucking. It was just my intensity and focus on this little kid was more than those shoulders could bear. And it was easy enough to cure."

As Jeff got older, his mother joined him for many activities. "I taught him to ski," Steiger says. "In addition to sports, I did what I could about generating an interest in art, which he carries on. He shared things with me that you might normally share with a sibling. Little things, like baking Christmas cookies. That's the sort of thing a mother could just let a bunch of kids loose on, but with us it was always our project, something we did together. I had the time, the inclination, and the fascination with the growing mind. I got a kick out of reading, and I got a kick out of playing sports on a very childish level. I had the time to do it, so I did it. It finally got to the point where he put his foot down and said, 'I'm not going to be a mamma's boy.' I had never thought of it that way."

Especially when only children are young, fretful parental attention can amount to an irritating level of protection. Marni Weil, an entrepreneur who owns an apparel company with her husband, chafed under what she thought was excessive attention as a child growing up in New York

City. "I was watched constantly," she remembers. "When I was little, my mother used to stare at me out the window. There was this one rock I used to love to sit on, and she'd invariably catch me and shout, 'Get off the rock, you'll catch a cold!' My father used to watch out the window as I got home from dates. I probably had my first sleep-over when I went to college. No, wait, I did go away to camp. I always thought it would be better to have a sibling to share this intensity or protection. I felt stifled. I was spoiled with anxieties." How did it ultimately affect her? "It made me rebel and be free."

Flip Spiceland, a meteorologist in Atlanta for the Cable News Network, also found that the attention had a double edge. "I really was the center of their universe. There's no doubt about it. I can never remember once having been left with a baby-sitter. I remember I always had a difficult time learning to tell time. I never had to. If I had to be anywhere, someone came and got me and took me to the place I was supposed to be."

Spiceland's parents were enthusiastic about all his activities. His father was manager of the baseball team and president of the Little League. His mother was a den mother and president of the PTA. "When I got older, I did feel that there was a bit of pressure involved in being an only child," he says. "I had an ulcer when I was twelve years old. Oddly enough, they make no bones about being very driving and pushy parents. They have no qualms about it. They were totally involved in all of my activities, probably more so than I was. I had to somehow be all things to all people. I was the only one there to fulfill all of Mom and Dad's dreams of what they wanted in life."

Margaret Truman Daniel, the daughter of Bess and Harry Truman, is an interesting example of an only child who made the attention work for her. As a girl, she was over-protected and kept close to home while growing up in Independence, Missouri. Bess would take "Maggie" south in the winter for months at a time, leaving poor Harry behind, because she thought the warmer climate was better for her daughter's health. When Bess and Harry were in Washington, Bess would leave very specific instructions concerning everything from food to chaperones.

When she became First Daughter, Margaret Truman was apparently well-equipped to deal with the scrutiny that might overwhelm another. While it is a sign of the times that presidential offspring Ron Reagan can cavort on *Saturday Night Live* in his BVDs, Margaret Truman seized the spotlight with more refinement but certainly as much boldness. In 1947, she made her debut as a professional coloratura soprano with the Detroit Symphony Orchestra. Never before had an untried artist been given such serious publicity. A 1951 *Time* magazine cover story on Margaret related: "Friends suspect that Bess Truman never wanted Margaret to sing in public, that it was indulgent Harry who gave his daughter encouragement."

Indeed, a glimpse of "indulgent" Harry shows that he did give his daughter unconditional support. In *Bess W. Truman,* the biography of her mother, Margaret writes about what her father did when *Washington Post* critic Paul Hume panned her performance. "Without saying a word to me or Mother, who would have stopped him, he dashed off a note to Mr. Hume that told him in very Trumanesque language what he thought of him. Among other picturesque suggestions, he said Mr. Hume sounded like 'an eight ulcer man on a four ulcer job with all four ulcers working.' Dad had one of the White House servants mail it for him, thus circumventing his staff, who also tried to persuade him to think over such letters before he sent them. Mr. Hume promptly released the letter to the press, and the hullabaloo temporarily knocked the Korean War off the front pages." A few days later, Harry wrote a note saying, "I've been accused of putting my 'baby' who is the 'apple of my eye' in a bad position. I don't think that is so. She doesn't either, thank the Almighty."

Since only children spend more time with adults than children with brothers and sisters, they tend to become verbally adept at an early age. They also tend to spend more time alone, reading books. As a result, only children are often precocious. Judy Anderson-Wright, an only child and a specialist in early childhood education at Metropolitan State College in Colorado, says that parents of only children spend more time stimulating them. "That time often shows up in language and more expressive language," she notes. "As these children sit and talk to adults, they mimic adult language patterns. That translates into skills in learning how to read and write." The only children she sees tend to be a bit ahead in motor skills, too, partly because of opportunities to take gymnastics and participate in other types of activities. Concludes Anderson-Wright: "I see only children having their little acts together more."

Indeed, there are many famous prodigies who were only children: Van Cliburn, the pianist, and Jean-Paul Sartre, the French philosopher, to name two of the more famous ones. Only children, of course, do not have any monopoly on genius; nor are only children guaranteed to be bright. But statistically, they do seem to be ahead of their peers.

For most only children, a major advantage is academic. In general, the smaller the family, the brighter the children. Lillian Belmont and Francis A. Marolla surveyed the scores of over 386,000 Dutch men who were born between 1944 and 1947, who took the Dutch military exam. They found that the first child in a family of two got the highest scores, while the last child in a family of nine got the lowest. Even controlling for social class, the researchers found that the family size had a major impact on how well the individual scored on intelligence tests. The firstborn in an affluent family of two would score higher than the firstborn in an equally affluent family of four.

Robert Zajonc and colleagues at the University of Michigan's Institute for Social Research began studying intelligence tests in the U.S. to figure out why firstborns do better. They developed what is known as the confluence model, a mathematical equation that estimates the intelligence quotient of a family. Zajonc sets the parents' intelligence level at 100; a newborn's level at 0. If a family is comprised of two adults, the intelligence level is 100 plus 100, divided by 2, to equal 100. Add a new baby, and the equation changes to 100 plus 100 plus 0, divided by 3, to equal 67. When another baby comes along, the family's intelligence quotient sinks even lower (100 + 100 + 15 for the older child + 0 = 215; divided by 4, the family's score is 54). Thus, both the number of children and the spacing contribute to the family's overall intelligence. Zajonc supports his theories with evidence from the Scholastic Aptitude Test (SAT) scores. In 1976, when baby boomers and their siblings were preparing for college, the average score was 445. Back in 1963, though, when family size was smaller, the average score was 490. As Zajonc predicted, SAT scores have risen again since 1976, as family size has decreased.

Onlies tend to do better in school than their counterparts with siblings. Project TALENT, a research survey begun in 1960, with follow-ups one, five, and eleven years later, tracked the attitudes, abilities, and achievements of 4.5 percent of the four hundred thousand American high school students across the country. Although Project TALENT was not devised specifically as an only-child study, John Claudy and his colleagues at the Research Associates of Palo Alto analyzed a subsample: all the families with one or two children. Because the children were all from intact, two-parent homes, of similar socioeconomic status, this study is one of the most reliable sources of information on only children. Project TALENT found that onlies scored better than children with siblings on twenty-five out of thirty-two cognitive tests. The researchers concluded: "The onlies in this sample appear to be at least equal and probably superior to those from two-child families in terms of cognitive and intellectual functioning."

Being around adults a lot can give a child a real head start, at least with superficial knowledge and wit. Talk-show host Dick Cavett, who even as an adult seems to personify precocity, remembers: "I was expected to be part of my parents' group. I felt more conversant with adults than with kids my own age. I didn't feel out of place being the kid with a group of adults. Occasionally I remember making what must have been very precocious remarks. One day, for instance, this guy said: 'I remember seeing Jim's sister when she was just a babe in arms.' I said: 'And now she's a babe in someone else's arms.' I remember that everyone looked at me as if to say, what came out of this baby over here? I remember having that kind of effect: Wow, where did *that* come from? Did that come out of him? If I had had brothers and sisters, the three of us probably would have been put off somewhere."

Spending time with parents can also allow a child experiences that are not always open to people of their age group. Elizabeth Clark has lasting memories of going with her mother to fashion shows and having lunch at Neiman-Marcus while she was still in high school. Her father, who is a private investigator, used to take her on cases with him. Says she: "I always thought it was kind of neat. I got to go places, do things, be exposed to what's out there. I never had to compete for attention. And they didn't try to shelter me."

The benefits can last a lifetime for those only children who relished their special relationships with adults. Says Ann Fisher: "When people ask if I liked being an only child, I say that it has gotten me a long way. I was comfortable with adults, poised. It opened another age group to me." Harriet Benson believes that she benefited from the fact that her mother worked. "I really feel that I have been part of the working world ever since my mother was dragging me to parties at her office," she says. "I certainly never had any difficulty with adults. I remember when my mother took me to parties, she would remind me ahead of time who everyone was, the names of their spouse and children, and what we should talk about. I felt I was well-trained for social amenities like that from an early age."

There can be problems, however, when an only child spends too much time with adults. The impressive vocabulary and pseudosophistication can be more attractive to adults than to children. Kathy Gay, an IBM manager in Maryland, has strong negative feelings about having been an only child because of what she calls a "little adult" syndrome. "I never saw my friends, except at school," she recalls. "I was trained to be a little brain-child, teacher's pet, that sort of thing. Everything was focused on being a little adult, not whatever was normal for my age. It was always: How soon can you grow up? How soon can you work? My parents had me selling things when I was in sixth grade." Gay says there was not a lot of time, nor a lot of emphasis, placed on peer relationships. "I wasn't allowed to have friends into the house," she recalls. "There were always other things to do. I was supposed to be working on my homework, or taking piano lessons, or going to meetings with my mother."

Gay feels that there was simply too much adult-oriented attention. "There was a lot of intellectual stuff. I did happen to be very smart and they played that up. There were a lot of trips, a lot of museums, but no children's activities. I was the little wonder-child. Of course, you're around adults a lot and start parroting things. You do learn a lot. So you get smarter and you start sounding like an adult. Other kids saw me as too much of an adult. I related better to the teachers than I did to my peers. That doesn't go well with school kids. Now I resent it even more. I say there's no reason to do that to a child. Let them have fun. There's plenty of time to be responsible."

The existential philosopher Jean-Paul Sartre had savage recollections of his prodigious youth. In his autobiography, *The Words,* Sartre describes how, after his father's death, he and his mother went to live with his stern and demanding grandfather. "I'm a promising poodle; I prophesy," he writes. "I make childish remarks, they are remembered, they are repeated to me. I learn to make others. I make grown-up remarks. I know how to say things 'beyond my years' without meaning to."

Books, not surprisingly, were Sartre's first friends. After he started to write, his mother lavished encouragement on him. He recalls: "She would bring visitors into the dining-room so that they could surprise the young creator at his school-desk. I pretended to be too absorbed to be aware of my admirers' presence. They would withdraw on tiptoe, whispering that I was too cute for words, that it was too-too charming." If he complained to his mother about his insular life, she would remind him of all his advantages. Sartre concluded: "A spoiled child isn't sad; he's bored, like a king. Like a dog."

Still, Sartre felt a certain predestination to be extraordinary. "My family . . . had told me again and again that I was a gift of heaven," he wrote, "that I had been eagerly awaited, that I was indispensable to my grandfather, to my mother. I no longer believed it, but I did continue to feel that one is born superfluous unless one is brought into the world with the special purpose of fulfilling an expectation."

The parent who wants the very best for his or her child is nothing new. Creating a better life for one's sons and daughters is a time-honored tradition. When there is only one child, the aspirations may be even more pointed and poignant. Only children can be empowered by their parents' expectations to become high achievers (see Chapter Seven). But there is a downside: Expectations can become a burden.

Michelle, thirty-six, an only child who lives in Indiana, recounts: "I think my mom must have thought I was born with magical powers. She expected me to be tall and pretty, to go out there and do all the things she hadn't done and to really do them in a big way. When I was a teenager and in my early twenties, she finally had to admit that I was not going to do what she wanted me to do. I think she was very disappointed."

Formerly in an administrative job for the federal government in Arizona, Michelle is now going back to school to "get a piece of paper that says I know how to do what I know how to do." What did her mother expect of her? "I think she wanted me to go out and marry well and wear white gloves and have the particular kind of life she had wanted for herself," Michelle muses. "I've not to this day really figured out what she wanted. She never said exactly what it was. She just told me what I had not done."

Only children who are pushed toward perfection may grow up with the sense that nothing is good enough. Robin Bruna, a retired teacher in Kentucky, recalls the rigor of being brought up by her mother and aunt. "I had lessons, lessons, lessons," she says. "My mother made me learn the piano. I was not talented but determined. I graduated as valedictorian of my high school class, which wasn't hard to do with thirty graduates. A few weeks later, my mother found out that someone in the next town had graduated with a higher average and told me that I hadn't done so well."

But sometimes parental expectations are not particularly lofty. Mary Kay Shaw, an administrator for the Mount Holyoke College Alumnae Association in Massachusetts, felt that her parents simply needed her to be happy. She says: "I was an only child through default. My parents lost two other children. I had this feeling that I was never allowed to be sick because it panicked my parents. So I came through on the surface being happy, knowing that if I wasn't happy it threw my parents into a tizzy."

Many only children come to realize that their very existence is essential to their parents. Dick Cavett muses: "I wonder if only children think about death, in the sense that if they died that would be it for their parents. A guy died of polio in high school, and people kept saying, 'Oh, and he was their only child.' And I seem to remember thinking: If I died of polio and my parents had another child, it wouldn't be so bad, they wouldn't mind so much if I died? Is that what they're saying? Do only children feel a real obligation to stay alive?"

*   *   *

Given the ways parents put their only child first, the natural question is: Do only children always put themselves first? It is at the root of the idea that only children are spoiled and selfish. Again, the answer depends on the temperament of parent and child. "I probably think of myself first," admits Ruth Brine, the retired editor and mother of three children. "I try to have good manners, but basically I think of myself first. But maybe in a family where there are three or four children, they think of themselves first even more strongly."

For every only child who exploits the advantages, there are probably many more who feel that they must live up to their privileges. Indeed, spoiling tends to be in the eyes of the beholder. To some people, a spoiled child is one with too many toys. Or too much attention. Or too many opportunities. Judy Anderson-Wright has a different definition. "A spoiled child is a child who doesn't know any boundaries or limits," she says.

"People might say that I was spoiled," declares Renée Franklin, an only child and mother of an only child. "Well, someone said to me recently, 'Children should be spoiled.' What you're doing is giving the child extra-special love, care, and attention because this child is very precious to you." Adds Robin Bruna, the retired teacher who is an only child as well as the mother of one daughter: "When people say how spoiled we are, I tend to disagree. Unless people have a child very late in life, I think in most cases, parents of only children are stricter and observe more."

At least that is how Bruna brought up her only child, Lynne Humkey. "She did push me in certain things," Humkey recalls. "She did make me take piano lessons. I had to be kind of a well-rounded person. Her attitude was try everything, then you can pick and choose what you really like and stick with that. This was true even in teaching me to eat all the foods. I wasn't allowed to leave the table until I had eaten everything on my plate. Her theory was that you never knew where you were going to go and have to eat something you weren't accustomed to. I remember at one church dinner, one boy refused to eat chili, and another refused to have anything but a Coke. I went home to my mother and said, 'I'm glad you made me eat everything.' "

Charles Pelton, a journalist in San Francisco who emigrated to this country from Great Britain when he was seven, points out that it is up to parents to decide whether they will spoil a child. "I was lucky because I didn't have the attitude of being spoiled," he says. "When I went on a trip to Europe, my parents told me to save the money and they would support my going away. I mean, they were scared out of their minds. I scooped ice cream and was pretty enterprising and had enough money to travel around Europe and North Africa the year after I finished high school. They supported me by buying any clothes I needed, my knapsack, and my sleeping bag. But I had to pay for the rest of my expenses."

Spoiling also depends on the temperament of the child. "I'm absolutely everything to my father," says Tina Laskaris, a graphic artist living in Virginia. "I grew up in Jamestown, New York, not exactly the place of opportunity. My father was a bartender at a country club and had a lot of very wealthy friends. So I had access to lots of swimming pools and got lots of expensive presents. When I graduated from high school, my father bought me a car. I'm spoiled, perhaps, but I don't take advantage of my parents."

While most only children speak gratefully of privileges and possessions, some were embarrassed by their riches. Laura Stein-Stapleford, the public relations consultant in

Williamsburg, Virginia, found that as she got older the advantages were a disadvantage. "I grew up with two parents
who didn't have that much when they were growing up,"
she explains. "One was the eldest of six. The other was the
middle of three. There was never much money for them to
have what they wanted. So because they had only one child,
they had a lot more disposable income to spend on things.
Also, I grew up during the fifties and sixties when everybody was making money and spending money like it was
going out of style. I always had everything my mother
wanted when she was growing up. And I got everything my
father had wanted. Not only did I have a wardrobe that
wouldn't stop, I also had a car before I had a driver's license. All I had to do was mention, 'gee, wouldn't it be nice
to have . . .' and my wishes were taken care of."

Although she relished the cornucopia as a child, she now
acknowledges that there are pitfalls to plenty. "It was like
I always had to prove something to other people, maybe it
was more to myself," she muses. "If I was successful, I'd get
no credit because people would say, 'Of course, she was
born with a silver spoon in her mouth, her parents did everything they possibly could to grease the skids so that she'd
do well.' Yet, had I turned into a rock-throwing hippie, they
would have said, 'Of course, what can you expect of someone who had everything handed to her on a silver platter.'
I was in a no-win situation. I was their justification, the next
generation, the heir apparent. I was spoiled rotten. Sometimes I wonder how I turned out to be halfway decent at all."

There are other ways that material advantages can back-
fire. Ruth Ainslie, the Manhattan lawyer, recalls that she
always knew there would be financial backing for anything
she did—but the backing often turned out to be a back-
handed compliment. She never felt that she was given privi-

leges on her own merits. "They would tell me, 'If there were more of you, we couldn't afford to send you to this expensive camp.' It wasn't like, 'You're wonderful, so we're sending you to this wonderful camp.' It was the same with college. It was, 'You can go to the college of your choice, but if we had more children, you'd be going to Ohio State.' It enabled me to do a lot of things I might otherwise not have done. But, in a sense, it was a negative thing. I shouldn't feel too good about anything."

A TALE
Betty Rollin, early fifties, television correspondent and writer, New York City:

I'm a Pollyanna—one of those "it's for the best" people. So I was determined to see the advantages of being an only child, and I think my mother was, too. That may say more about our dispositions than the facts.

Sometimes being an only child made me feel bad. For example, I grew up in an Irish-Catholic neighborhood in Yonkers. Not only was I the only only child, but the other kids had five and six brothers and sisters. I felt not just only and lonely, but also unusual, which is not what a kid wants to feel. Plus, we were Jewish. It added to this feeling of being different.

I had my own room. The Irish kids across the street thought I was the luckiest girl in the world. But I thought, gee, they're talking to each other and playing games at night. I thought these kids who had live-in playmates were so fortunate. Yet, while the Irish kids across the street were playing with each other and having a wonderful time, I was sitting in my room doing something—making pictures or reading a book. It made me feel a little lonely, but I don't think it's an accident that I wound up a writer.

I was very aware as I was growing up that my parents didn't have much money. And a major portion of what money they had was spent on me. I knew perfectly well that if there had been a sibling, it would have been a different story. As a result of being the only one and having all these things, I felt we were rich. That was good, I think. I felt privileged. And I've always had a secure feeling about money.

The whole thing was so intense. I was it. My parents were very child-oriented. I was the focus of their lives. That never really changed, even when I went to college. I had an analyst once who said: "A lot of people think they're crazier than they are or have had experiences that make them more unusual than they are, but when you tell me that your mother moved next door to Sarah Lawrence, I knew you had a problem." The focus part was so intense. My father went along.

I did a lot of hiding. I concealed men I was living with. I thought they couldn't bear it, because there was no other "good" sibling. The hiding makes you crazy, and it's something you must do. You feel, incorrectly, that they'll fall apart.

I felt in a way that I had to be both sexes. Of course, it was completely unspoken. Sometimes I think if I had had a brother, he would have been the one who had to accomplish, and I would have been the one who had to be domestic. My mother denies this. But the fact is that because I was an only child, I was pushed toward both roles: that I was to get married and have children someday; and that I was also to have a career, to accomplish, to be somebody. In a sense, given the times, before the women's movement, I'm grateful. That was a bonus of being an only child that I didn't realize until I was forty years old.

My identity and who I decided to be had a lot to do with my mother and reacting to her and what she wanted from me. I was confused because I got double messages. Be independent. Be dependent. Be exceptional. Do what everyone else does. Yet, ultimately, she was a great sport about my not having children. I married when I was thirty-six, so by the time I got married they were just so glad I got married. My first husband and I couldn't have natural children. Besides, I just wasn't one of those women who had a great desire. Once it was clear, she never made me feel bad about it. And I know she must have felt bad. My first husband had an adopted child from a previous marriage, and my mother became that child's grandmother. It was kind of funny. Even after the divorce, she still saw this child. She'd smile and introduce him: "This is Matthew; he's Betty's ex-husband's child by his first wife."

When I wrote a piece about why motherhood is overrated, my mother was absolutely miserable. She took it personally. As my writing career got better and better and it was clear that I

wasn't going to have a baby, I thought I had satisfied my parents by having a career. But I think
that my mother felt that if she had been a better
mother, I would have felt more positive about
having children. Sometimes I wonder whether
the fact that my mother was such an intense
mother caused me to feel that I could never mea-
sure up to that standard, so I'd better not try. I'm
not sure if that's true; it's just something I question sometimes.

I heard her say to other people: "It's so wonderful to have a daughter." She'd tell me that it was
the major thing in her life, to have a child. Although I've described the intensity in a slightly
negative way, an aspect of it was good. Focusing
on a child is not such a bad thing, especially compared to the opposite, which you see much more.
I do stories all the time about children who are
born and nobody much notices them after that.
The attention, the love, the flattery, were good. It
didn't make me a monster. Surely, I'm self-centered. I write about myself a lot; I think about
myself a lot. But people tell me I'm a good listener,
and I'm intensely interested in other people. I have
good relationships and close friendships. In a way,
I think I had so much attention that I can afford
not to have the attention on me now.

My mother got from me what she wanted. She
said so. I was always pushing and pulling, rebel-
ling on the one hand and giving her what she
wanted on the other. And I think I came full circle
to realize that just because my mother wanted
some things for me, it didn't mean that I didn't

want them, too. For instance, I wound up marrying someone she thought was the most wonderful man who ever lived. She adored my husband. And so do I. I don't think I could have married someone she adored early on. I was still struggling to separate myself.

I think one feels obliged to please these parents; you're all they have. On the other hand, you feel you have to please yourself because you're a human being and you're all that you have. I think that's the conflict of being an only child. There was certainly a period in which I felt a strong pull to be what my parents wanted me to be. Although that was never exactly defined, I had an idea of what that was. On the other hand, I had just as strong a pull to be what I wanted, although I didn't know what that was either. I just knew it had to be different. Then it turned out, because my parents were good people with good values, what they wanted from me was what I wanted from me. A lot of my own peace comes from the fact that I was all my parents had and I pleased them—and I pleased myself. If I had done one and not the other, I think I would have been in torment.

four

SIBLINGS

AND

SOCIAL

SKILLS

M_y brother was a dog. I know that some people might say the same thing. But mine had black-and-white fur. The first brother was a Boston Terrier named Torgie after an outfielder for the Red Sox. He was actually older than I and had been named before I was born. Otherwise, his name probably would have been Tuggs or Cupcake or something less sportif.

Torgie and I were very close. He walked me to the lane every day to see me off on the school bus. He waited by the door for my return. We went sledding together. We often embraced. If you've ever seen a Boston Terrier, you know they're not cuddly, long-eared "dawgs." Torgie had a mature and dignified demeanor; he was a suitable companion. Torgie's death, when he was twelve and I was ten, was very traumatic. I felt my best friend had died. I played "Smoke Gets in Your Eyes" over and over on the stereo.

Then along came André (my choice of a name), a silver poodle. Andy (his nickname) was subjected to a lot of dress-up. At Christmastime, poor thing, he had to put on a felt Santa Claus outfit that came with a gray beard. I even bought him some little red rubber boots. He was a pretty good sport. He'd tolerate his costume for at least fifteen or twenty minutes.

Andy and I used to fight quite a bit. I found it very entertaining. One night we were really in the thick of it. I was pushing him around in the living room, and he was pouncing back on me. At one point he inadvertently, I think, grabbed the sleeve of my oxford cloth shirt and tore a hole in it. At that point, my aunt stepped in. "We got you this dog so you'd have someone to love," she said to me. I had no idea that fighting precluded love. Andy and I knocked it off.

I can't remember yearning for a sister. I suppose, like most little girls, I fantasized about having a big brother who eventually would fix me up with dates or protect me from bullies. Yet, I don't think I was overly enamored of the idea of brothers and sisters. One girl I used to play with had a sister who was four years older who would not give us the time of day. She was as dismissive as a princess. Another friend had a younger brother and sister, who would follow us like bumbling detectives. My friend and I were always giving them the slip.

I was never allowed to sleep over at friends' houses, so I never got to see any after-hours sibling activity. That great bonding institution, the slumber party, was off limits to me. My aunt believed that children should sleep in their own beds. The first time I was ever allowed to spend a night away from my family was when I went off to visit colleges my senior year in high school. I was looking forward to being on my own.

When I did start my freshman year at Mount Holyoke College, I ended up rooming with another only child. This was a relief, despite the fact that we were very different. Holly went to bed early; I was a night owl. She liked the window open; I liked it shut. She was extroverted and popular. I liked to spend a lot of time alone. Like the opposites in the Gershwin song, we could have called the whole thing off (at least in the second semester). But we were actually thrilled to find each other. We shared clothes, records, road trips. We welcomed intimacy, but we understood the notion of privacy.

One day when we were in a store shopping, the saleswoman asked us *if we were sisters. Since I was a good four inches taller and we were the same age, I was taken aback. Then we thought about it. Why, yes, we both had brown hair, light complexions, and a similar way of talking. We could pass as sisters! By then, we knew we would be friends for life. In my opinion, this was better than having a sister. We had freely chosen each other.*

People seem to think that growing up with a brother or sister deserves a *Good Housekeeping* seal of social approval. Only children tend to be considered odd, or socially maladjusted, because they allegedly haven't learned the important lessons that siblings can teach.

But what, really, are sibling relationships like? And what do they teach people? In their book, *The Sibling Bond,* psychologists Stephen P. Bank and Michael D. Kahn discuss the ties between siblings. When siblings are of the same age and sex, for instance, they have what is called "high access" to each other. They often go to the same schools and know the same people. They may even share a bedroom. If the age difference is four years or more, however, siblings tend not to be as close. Bank and Kahn maintain: "As lived by each individual who is a brother or a sister, the sibling experience dictates some of the grandest and some of the meanest of human emotions."

Let's take a look at some of the grand moments. There is much truth to the value of the sibling bond, to the idea that blood is thicker than water. There are plenty of brothers and sisters who stand by each other throughout life, who evoke memories of happy days gone by, who embody the same family genes and traditions. Siblings can be an elegant safety net. I know many people who turn first to their brother or sister for help—in borrowing money, sharing their sorrows, or, even better, in seeking fun. Anita Fiorello, the mother of one child, recalls that the biggest advantage of having a sibling was in the playing. "My brother and I," says Fiorello, "had these very involved, complicated games that we played. They went on by the hour and they didn't involve or need adults. Although, of course, we had many times when we didn't want to speak to each other at all."

But sibling bonds also can be glorified. Not everyone comes from the proverbial big, happy family. Kathy Viscardi Martin, a lawyer in Rochester, New York, was one of seven children and is the mother of one. "Sometimes people are close to their brothers and sisters," she says. "And sometimes they're not. As one of seven, I remember that my mother physically just didn't have enough energy. My feeling is why have a second child and sacrifice my first for someone I don't know. I don't buy this notion of the second magical playmate."

The emphasis on the good of the family can be stifling to some of its members. One friend of mine, who is in her late sixties, grew up on a Minnesota farm as one of six children. She does not have a lot of fond memories about her childhood or her brothers and sisters. "I was looking through a photo album one day," she says, "and I realized that the only picture of me alone was at my high school graduation. When I asked my mother about it, she said, 'Why, we couldn't afford to take a picture of you all by yourself!' " After marrying, this woman chose to adopt two children rather than to have her own "because there were already so many children who needed a home."

Even if a family can give enough attention to everyone, there may be niches that children get pushed into: the scholar, the athlete, the beauty, the clown. Or, even worse, they may be expected to follow the firstborn's lead. Anthropologist Mary Catherine Bateson notes: "Some cultures have a theory of multi-child families in which there are certain predefined roles for people. My husband is Armenian, and I've always been struck by the notion that in Armenian families there is one who carries on the spiritual heritage, there's the black sheep, and there's a responsible person who goes and makes money. Similarly, there's the notion that one daughter is going to be beautiful and one daughter is going to be ugly. What I hear more from Americans is an expectation of similarity. If you go to the school in which your older brother was the football star, everybody says, 'Why aren't you a football star?' There is a sense of being stereotyped in expectations to be like your siblings."

Not measuring up can be as painful as being pigeonholed. Marilyn Malkin, mother of one child and a literary agent in New York City, remembers: "I had a brother who was two years younger. I adored my brother, but I always felt that he was better looking, smarter, more athletic and the favored child. I felt I was in his shadow. When we were little, he was my best friend. Strangely enough, as adults we're not close."

Then, of course, there is overt sibling rivalry, a problem as old as Cain and Abel. It can manifest itself in simple, mindless aggression. My husband, who has a great relationship with his sister, can still remember how terrified he was as a little boy when she held him, almost to the point of suffocation, under the bedcovers. Another friend recalls throwing his younger sister out of a rowboat, despite the fact that he knew she couldn't swim. He is not proud of himself. As adults, these people scratch their heads in puzzlement over such nasty childhood antics.

Some of these antics continue, however, throughout life. One of my friends got married several years ago. It was a great party, with plenty of singing and dancing. By the end of the evening, however, he and his brother were engaged in a fistfight. It seemed pretty bizarre, until we considered the continuing rivalry. There are, in fact, many notable examples of brothers and sisters who undermine one another throughout life: Billy Carter, signing on with Libyan lobbyists while Jimmy's pushing human rights; Donald Nixon taking dubious loans while Tricky Dicky is trying to clean up his image; Dear Abby and Ann Landers, the celebrated Friedman twins, Eppie and Popo, who as adults speak to the world but not to each other. (In her book, *Eppie,* Margo Howard speculates that her mother always wanted a singular identity. "If I thought it was intriguing that there were, in a way, two of my mother," writes Howard, "she found it appealing that I would go through life alone. With me, she could see what it must be like to be a single child, set apart, sharing nothing.") Sibling rivalry is a cross an only child never has to bear.

Despite daily evidence that sibling relationships can be problematic, many only children fantasize about what they might be like. Only children can be very idealistic about the sibling they never had. When researchers Sharryl Hawke and David Knox asked their sample of only children whether they had ever wanted a sibling, 64 percent said they had. A third reported that they had wanted a sibling most when they were in elementary school, a time when their friends were acquiring little brothers and sisters.

One only child now in his forties knows that somewhere in the world he has a half-brother. "My father had a child from his first marriage who would be much older than I am—if he is still alive," he explains. "My father has reason to believe he's not. But I sometimes fantasize about that, the idea of trying to hunt down my long-lost brother. Maybe

I'm sentimentalizing. I do it in the face of all the evidence. My wife and her sister don't have a civil word to say to one another. And my father himself, after not seeing a brother of his for fifty years—after the First World War, the family was dispersed in Dostoyevskian fashion—went to Israel about ten years ago to see the long-lost brother. He came back to report that he never liked the son-of-a-bitch then, and he doesn't like the son-of-a-bitch now. So there's all this empirical evidence that adult sibling relationships are not undiluted bliss. Yet, I still think it would be very nice to find that long-lost brother."

It is natural to dream about all the good things a family can be. Holly Mak, thirty-five, a banker in Washington, D.C., and the mother of two, speaks longingly of an ideal family life. "I always looked at big families and thought: I wish I had brothers and sisters around because it seems so friendly and warm. I just liked the bigger family atmosphere. I think what I missed by being an only child was the sense of a larger family, everyone looking out for one another. I've always felt this superficially—and I may feel it deep down—that being an only child was not that happy an experience. I realize that you can have brothers and sisters and not relate to them. Maybe I have an idealized view of families."

Only children have very strong ideas about what siblings could have been—everything from allies to role models. On a very basic level, many only children wish for companionship. Laura Stein-Stapleford, who talked earlier about the material advantages she had, always wanted someone to share them. "My parents would buy these games for me and most of the time they just sat there because they required two people to play," says Stein-Stapleford. "Playing 'Go Fish' or 'War'—all those games are set up for two or more to play. The vacations of my school friends—maybe up to a rented cabin in Wisconsin—might not have been as grandiose as mine. But it always seemed to me that they were having more fun. Whether it was true or not, I always perceived other people as having more fun because they had people to do it with."

Kathy Gay, the IBM executive, says, "When you're an only child you don't have anyone else to confide in. There's nobody to fight back with. If you have a brother or sister, you've got someone to collaborate with, you've got a buddy automatically. Everybody's got their complaints growing up, but I think if you're an only child, you can get too introspective because there's nobody there to affirm your feelings. Nobody's going through what you're going through."

For only children who ache for a sibling, there is no real replacement. Ralph Bermudo, an accountant who is in his late twenties, emigrated from Cuba with his parents when he was only eight months old. Like many Cuban immigrants, Ralph's parents stopped at one child, perhaps because of the stress of coming to a new country and starting over. Ralph has a cousin, also an only child, with whom he is very close. "I was the brother she didn't have, and she's the sister I didn't have," says Ralph. But close as they were, Ralph does not feel she was an adequate substitute for the real thing. "It's different," he explains. "You don't wake up in the same house at Christmas. You don't share the same parents. My kids will probably have uncles, but I won't really be an uncle myself."

Ralph, like many other only children, believes that siblings help one to grow up. "Brothers and sisters are kind of representative of the world out there. When you don't have them, you have to figure things out on your own. You have to make more of an effort to deal with other people and accept them as they are."

Frederick Golden, a science writer and editor living in San Francisco, believes that having a sister could have made his relations with the opposite sex a little easier. "All of growing up is practice, an experiment in how to live your life," he says. "The fact that you're growing up in this hothouse atmosphere means that you may flourish at the time, but later on it probably does affect you. My relationships with women are probably guided by my relationship with my mother. I could have used an influence apart from that. I would have liked to have had a sister."

Yet many only children are philosophical about what they may have lost—or gained—by not having a sibling. "My father informs me that I begged for a baby brother or sister," recalls Lenore Rogers, a teacher in Steilacoom, Washington. "If it had been a red wagon, I would have asked for a red wagon. Everyone had baby brothers and sisters, so that's what I asked for. Then I went on to roller skates."

Only children who are comfortable with themselves tend to look upon their status as natural, even ordained. In *Five Boyhoods,* John Updike wrote about his childhood in Shilling, Pennsylvania, where he lived in a house with his mother, father, and grandparents during the Depression. "I do not remember ever feeling the space for a competitor within the house," he writes. "The five of us already there locked into a star that would have shattered like crystal at the admission of a sixth." Dick Cavett claims he was not aware of wanting a brother or sister. "It never occurred to me that my parents would want anyone else," he says. "My guess is that it never occurred to me that they would dare have anyone but me."

There are even only children who consider the absence of siblings advantageous. Jim Shaw, the assistant dean of the

College of Arts and Sciences at the University of Massachusetts, says: "I remember at some point consciously thinking
that I was glad I didn't have a brother or sister because
they'd be the people who did it right. At least this way there
wasn't any invidious comparison—just me versus perfection. Otherwise, it would have been me versus perfection
versus Harold or Susie. That seemed to me an advantage.
When I was growing up, I didn't know a brother or sister
who had a kind word to say about a sibling. I never saw
that I was missing anything except a headache or an upset
stomach."

Susan Shwartz, the writer who felt so hurt by the spoiled-
brat label, admits that she cannot approach the question of
brothers and sisters dispassionately because of all the adults
who swarmed at her as a child, asking if she wanted a
sibling. "I've seen brothers and sisters who don't get along
at all, who don't speak, who turn on one another, who
betray one another, and I would rather be an only child than
have that," she says. "As for wonderful relationships between brothers and sisters, I'm sure they exist. But I can't
miss what I haven't had."

Whether they feel they missed having siblings or not,
only children tend to be pretty hard on themselves when
they talk about social skills. Most only children, myself
included, believe that had they grown up with a sibling,
they would have learned how to deal with others sooner and
more smoothly. They feel that they are a bit slow sensing
the dynamics of peer relationships or learning the art of
negotiation.

John Updike, in reflecting on being an only child, says:
"The up side is surely undivided parental attention and love,
lending the child a self-confidence that may take him or her

far, or may lead him to bump up against the cruel world with a bigger bruise than usual. The down side is perhaps an unease or timidity in the rough-and-tumble of human contact."

In studying the social skills of only children, researchers have weighed in with mixed reviews. Project TALENT, the far-reaching study of American high school students, asked individuals to assess themselves in a number of areas, including sociability, sensitivity, and maturity. Each person had to rate himself on a scale of one to five on 150 statements, ranging from "I enjoy getting to know people," to "People seem to think I have good taste," to "I work better with ideas than things." Onlies and members of two-child families did not differ significantly on the questions of impulsiveness, leadership, self-confidence, or vigor. However, onlies did consider themselves more mature, cultured, sensitive, and tidy.

Students with one sibling, on the other hand, scored higher on sociability. Indeed, when Project TALENT researchers measured social life in terms of dating and intensity, only children did seem to be at a disadvantage. Children with a sibling generally began dating earlier and had more dates and a more active social life. At least at the high school level, there was some evidence that people with siblings actually do have more fun.

There are people who are natural social beings. But most of us, only children or not, usually work at acquiring good social skills. This process usually starts in earnest when we begin school. Many only children I spoke to remember how much they enjoyed going to school because of the opportunities to be with other children. Carmelita Thomson, the psychological therapist in Eugene, Oregon, grew up on a farm in Oklahoma during the middle of the Depression. "I had a fever, a desire to be with other children," she says. "Going to school made a big difference. I had some trouble learning how to play. Even as a young adult, it was hard learning how to just be loose. I think it was that I was very controlled, overly adult at a very early age."

Some only children really are shy and introverted. Carol Barron, a banker living in Tempe, Arizona, says, "I had a hard time interacting in groups. It took me a long time to come out of my shell. I was always the quiet one. All through school my teachers would say how quiet I was. I have a lot of friends now, but I find it hard to get really close to people. I'm not sure if that's because I'm an only child. But there's always a wall surrounding me." Beverly Agniel, thirty-seven, an administrative assistant living in Burbank, California, says, "I don't know if being an only child contributed to my being an introvert or if that's just my nature. I'm the type of person who will go to a party, and if I can sit comfortably with one person in the corner all night, I will, as opposed to being a mingler."

Ruth Brine remembers that she preferred not to talk when she was a child. "I remember one little girl saying, 'You've got to talk or I'll choke you,' " laughs Brine. "I wouldn't say a word. I remember walking to school reading a book, and I damned near got run over crossing the street. I came home from school and read and practiced my music." But Brine's shyness melted as she got older. "I first fell in love when I was fifteen. This was a boy who came from a big, Irish family who lived in a house that was always full of people. It was just as if I were visiting a foreign country. I couldn't get enough of it. I virtually moved out of my house and into his. My house seemed so sterile and quiet, even though Mother would have the whole football team over. I thought it was wonderful to be adopted by that big Irish family."

*   *   *

For every only child who is a shrinking violet, there are others who may be overeager. Charles Pelton remembers throwing himself into childhood friendships. "I think being an only child makes you a little socially backward for a year or two," he explains. "You're so busy trying to fill a sibling niche that you're not discovering the meaning of friendship. I was so interested in sharing daily experiences with people, that I just came on too strong. When I first started getting interested in girls, it was really difficult for me. They kept being sisters. I didn't want them to be. I wanted to kiss them and to make them girlfriends. It was because I had no same-age female role model. It was hard to figure out how to have a young woman in my life."

The teen years are tough for anyone. For an only child, they may be a time of uncertainty accompanied by a need to reach beyond family members for advice. Chelsea Coan, a teenager in Neenah, Wisconsin, says that one of the big problems is finding someone in whom you want to confide. "The biggest disadvantage to me about being an only child is that I don't always want to talk to my mom and dad," she says. "There are things I don't want them to know. I like to be a little secretive about things, but sometimes when you're an only child that's impossible. They want to know what you're doing all the time. Most of my friends do confide in brothers and sisters. Usually there's one particular brother or sister they're close to. I do talk to my friends. But I usually end up going to my parents."

While girls seem to feel comfortable talking about their problems with friends, many boys think that they will lose face if they confide in a buddy. One only child, who grew up in a tough neighborhood in the Bronx, describes the dilemma. "Not having an older brother or sister to teach you anything can be a problem because you don't have anybody to look to for sexual advice or advice about sports," he says. "It can be difficult. I didn't want to go to someone who was my peer and say, 'How do you play football?' I didn't have a father or a brother, so I started trying to figure out some of these things earlier. A boy would never go to his best friend and say, 'I'm going out with this girl, how do I do it?' A lot has to do with the environment you grow up in, of course. In a tough environment you would never, ever, consider doing that because everyone would make fun of you. In my particular case, it only motivated me to push myself more to learn how to do these things."

Clearly, only children come with all sorts of personalities. Whether they are shy or outgoing depends on many factors: temperament, interests, opportunities to make friends. Parents can play a pivotal role in helping a child acquire good social skills. When I was young, for instance, my aunt and I would drive to a neighborhood store to pick up extra grocery items. She always made me go inside to buy whatever it was we needed. At the time, I thought she was just being lazy. Later, she told me that she had pushed me into going into the store by myself so that I would overcome my shyness.

Psychologist Toni Falbo, herself an only child, remembers early days full of activity. "My parents were very careful in brokering experiences for me," she says. "They wanted to make sure I joined the Girl Scouts and Little League and played with friends. They signed me up for every imaginable organization from day one. It really encouraged my social participation. I didn't have periods of dull, lonely, passive times."

Many parents of only children say that they make a special effort to see that their child has companionship. Joan Starker, the urban planner in Portland, Oregon, says she sometimes feels like she's a social director. "I feel it is critical to have kids here," she says. "Sometimes I feel I have to be an administrator. You have to work hard at importing kids." Joan Steiger, the lawyer in Massachusetts, says, "Whenever we were doing a special thing or making a special trip, it turned out that it was always more fun if there was another child. Two children playing off each other is more fun than a child just playing off his parents. So we always had a kid in reserve for that. He was the son of a friend of ours and he was their third child. So they had done all the neat things, ad nauseum. They felt their son should do all this stuff, but they didn't particularly want to go through all of that again. He turned out to be a very, very close friend of Jeff's from nursery school on. I can't begin to tell you the things we did together."

Many only children remember how their parents welcomed their friends. "My parents were great about opening up the house," says Ellen Stone, an executive in San Francisco. "The kids across the street were like a second family. On holidays their family would not make a big to-do about things. So they would always come over to my house because we would have Easter-egg hunts." Stone says she is "basically a shy person." "My modus operandi was to stand back and observe and sort of go from there," she explains. "I developed a sixth sense of being able to read people very well."

Jonathan Bulkeley, a publishing executive in New York City, says his parents would usually let him invite a friend along on family vacation. "I had lots of friends in the neighborhood, who'd come over and play," he remembers. "My parents were very good about having people around. If we went away on a trip, I could bring a friend, which was nice. I wouldn't travel solo; I'd have a compatriot." Bulkeley's parents must have understood: They are both only children.

Anthropologist Mary Catherine Bateson, the mother of one daughter, believes that arranging for playmates is important. But she adds: "One of the great errors is to assume the playmate should be a peer. The whole school system is structured on age-mates. But families are structured on diversity of ages. When you're shopping around for another child for yours to spend time with, your child will learn more from one who is either older or younger. You can also avoid some comparison and competition that way."

There are some subtle ways that being an only child can affect the way a person deals with others, how he or she plays the game, if you will. A lot of only children discover with shock that people do not always tell the truth or mean what they say. While a person with a sibling learns this the first time he is tattled on, the only child may not learn about the deviousness of others until he is practically an adult. An only child can be quite naïve. To this day, I am the most gullible person in any room. My husband, a great practical joker, doesn't even bother to play any on me. It's so easy that it's no fun for him. I am very trusting. People are always innocent until proven guilty.

I am not alone. In his autobiography, *Yes I Can,* singer Sammy Davis, Jr., describes his early life, as the only child of a vaudeville entertainer. He would be on the road, performing with his father, for weeks at a time. Although he was a showbiz sophisticate, other children would make fun of him when he came home to Harlem, because he did not understand their world of bubble gum and baseball cards. One night as he and his father were playing a card game,

Davis caught him cheating. "Yes, son, I been doin' it for your own good," his father said. "I been cheatin' you so's to teach you the tricks of the game. That way when you grows up and I'm not around t'protect you there won't be nobody can suck you into a crooked game without you knowin' it. I'm doin' you a favor, son, so sit down and let's finish up."

Ann Beattie, forty, the author of the novels *Chilly Scenes of Winter, Falling In Place,* and *Love Always,* says she was an extremely shy child. Her novels, which frequently deal with disillusioned young adults who are trying to cope with a hostile world, reflect, in some ways, issues that she has faced. She was the only child of two "self-contained, very private people." As a young child, she had kidney surgery, which required hospitalization and "isolation from the world." Beattie admits that she grew up to be hypersensitive. "When I had to encounter the real world, I was quite surprised at people's random cruelty or preconceived notions," she says. "To this day, I'm quite taken aback when people who review my books are writing about my hairstyle. I had a very civilized upbringing. It was unrepresentative, I realize now, and I don't know what to do to get over it. In my family, I was considered wonderful unless something went wrong."

Because they grow up with fairly straightforward relations with the adult members of the household, only children tend to become straight shooters. When asked if she encountered any difficulties that she would attribute to being an only child, Lyn St. James, one of the leading race car drivers in the United States, focused on only one thing: What she calls "maneuverability." St. James maintains: "It becomes difficult to learn the tricks of the trade of living because you don't learn as much strategy for surviving. People get practice when there are other kids around. They learn how to get around their brother and sister, how to get what they want in this world. They have all this maneuverability. I'm so straightforward. If I want something, I say I want it. I usually accept a no—unless there's another way of getting it. I learned all this through business, but most people learn that as they grow up."

Only children may well be more candid than other people. William M. Kelly, Jr., retired publisher of *Money* magazine, recalls: "I didn't even realize I was an only child until I got to college." It was then that he first learned what diplomacy was all about. "I guess I had always accepted that I was candid and open," he says. "I'd lay what I thought on somebody, thinking I was doing the right thing. I remember the stunned looks I got when I went to college and joined a fraternity and met a whole new group of people. I got told where to go. I've never forgotten: You have to be sensitive to other people's feelings. Maybe only children don't have any reason to get that early on."

While only children have a well-documented need to excel, that sense of competition does not always extend to others. Joseph Mawson, a professor of forestry at the University of Massachusetts in Amherst, says he did not particularly miss having brothers or sisters. He notes, however, that to this day he thinks he's less competitive for it. "I used to play football, and I was a pretty good-sized individual," he says. "My coach once told me I'd never be a great football player. I didn't have the caliber for that. Looking back, he was right. I loved the sport, but it was only a game. I didn't have the desire to do bodily harm. I never developed a really keen sense of competition. I did my own thing. I still do. I think that may have something to do with being an only child."

Many only children tend to remain aloof from the fray.

One, who wished to remain anonymous, summed up her attitude toward others by saying: "I have always felt very comfortable being like the kid at the baseball game who decides to take his ball and go home. People may say, 'But we're doing this together.' And I say, 'Thanks a lot, but I don't need to.' "

It is interesting to note that only children seem to be underrepresented in politics and sports. This is not to say that only children cannot develop the required skills—New Jersey senator Bill Bradley and former Kentucky governor Martha Layne Collins, after all, are only children—but simply that only children do not tend to gravitate toward those activities. The Project TALENT study examined the activities preferred by only children. These high school students were asked about twenty-nine different pursuits, such as sports, hobbies, reading, and crafts. There were clear patterns. Only children clearly favored such pursuits as reading for pleasure, collecting stamps and coins, raising animals and having pets, performing (singing, acting, dancing), music, and photography. Children with a sibling, on the other hand, gravitated toward more robust, outdoor activities. They liked to play sports and learn practical skills, such as cooking, woodworking, and fishing. Indeed, if you look at only children who are well-known sports figures, they tend to take more individualistic roles: Joe Montana, the quarterback for the San Francisco '49ers; Ivan Lendl, one of the world's leading tennis players; Bret Saberhagen, the Cy Young Award-winning pitcher for the Kansas City Royals; and Christopher Bowman, the Olympic figure skater.

Many only children talk about the difficulties they had in dealing with conflicts or fights. Käthe Roth, a secretary with the Canadian government, thinks that you pick up those skills when you are forced to interact with peers—when you

cannot simply slam the door or go home. "I've had to un-
learn a lot of reactions I had as a child that were not appropriate for a child and certainly were not appropriate for an
adult," she admits. "For instance, the idea that if you have
a fight with someone, you can make up. That was a novel
concept for me. As a child, if I had a fight with someone, I
went home. If I never saw them again, that was fine.
Whereas if you have a sibling, and you have a fight with
them and you go to your room and close the door, you still
have to sit down with them at dinner. Ultimately, you have
to learn how to make up."

In his autobiography, *Giant Steps,* basketball player and
only child Kareem Abdul-Jabbar admits that he's not an
easy man to live with. "If you've got three brothers and one
afternoon you all hate each other, you've still got to sleep
together that night, and the next day they'll still be there;
you learn to deal with each other and develop a tolerance
and a way of accepting apologies and admitting mistakes.
An only child can retreat to his room and brood and never
have to abandon his hatred."

Only children who come from authoritarian households
may have a particular problem with negotiation. Robin
Smith of La Habra, California, makes an important point. "I
always felt I never had equals," she says. "I always had
superiors. Even though I had friends, you don't treat
friends—I don't think—the way you treat brothers and sisters. You can just be downright ornery and mean to your
brothers and sisters and they can't leave you. But you have
to be nice to your friends because they won't come back.
When you're growing up you always have superiors over
you, parents, teachers. But with your equals you always
have to kind of pussyfoot around. I don't think you develop
good fighting skills at all."

Of course, there are more subtle forms of negotiation that people must learn. Many only children go straight from being the precocious little kid at home to being the model student in school. Notes one only child, who is the father of two children: "You come out of the situation as a teenager or a young adult, and when you go to college or a job or whatever it is, the world hits you in the face and you have to learn some crucial lessons. You have to learn that you're not a hotshot. There are many people in the world who are one way or another more skillful, more proficient, more beautiful, more intelligent, more successful than you. That's as it should be. You have to learn to negotiate that situation in some healthy fashion. There's a greater chance that, with a sibling, you have to learn to wait. With our kids, there's always this constant kind of negotiation going on at home."

Kathy Gay found that after years of excelling at everything, it was something of a shock to get out into the business world and find out that there were a lot of other stars. "Learning to negotiate has been one of the hardest things for me at work," she says. "I think that if you had to work things out with a peer in your own house, you might have a little more practice and know how to negotiate with people when you grow up. I'm overcoming it. I've had to go through a lot of training to learn how to work with people. I'm very good at working with higher-ups. I'm very good at upper-management relationships, but not good at all with supervisory relationships. And I see that as a direct outpouring of my childhood. I'm getting better at peer-to-peer relationships because of a whole lot of training by my company. But it's never going to come naturally."

On some counts, however, only children come off socially ahead. University of Texas psychologist Toni Falbo conducted a study in the early 1970s to test cooperation. She put only and non-only children into groups together and asked them to do various tasks that required cooperation and competition, based on a game used by NASA. Afterward, she tested how well they liked one another and how they rated the others in terms of cooperation.

"Only children did very well," says Falbo. "They were probably more selfless, trusting, and trustworthy than people who had siblings." She found that only and non-only children initially used the same strategies to accomplish the tasks. However, she found that onlies were more likely to respond positively to a positive move by someone else. "Perhaps this is because only children, who grow up without competition from other children in the family, learn to trust the motives of other people," observes Falbo.

In addition to being trusting, only children often become people who enjoy sharing. Patricia Dalzell of Gloucester, Massachusetts, has found that her daughter Pammy is very generous with her possessions. "When you have brothers and sisters, you have more of a need to say, 'This is mine,'" says Dalzell, who had two siblings. "If you're an only child, you don't have to feel that you have to steal or hoard your own."

Sharing does not always come naturally. Sometimes it is a learned skill. Frances, a woman in her late fifties, recalls: "It was difficult for me to learn how to get along with other children. When I was about ten or eleven, we had a poor child stay with us for the summer. It was very difficult for me to share. I'd never had to wear hand-me-downs or anything like that. My parents were very angry with me. I wanted my things. I felt quite bad, too." Since then, Frances has worked harder at considering other people. "Things don't mean much to me now," she says. "I like to give things away. I don't have that need to have things. I guess it's because I had so much when I was young."

Bill Brennan, the producer who talked about how close he was to his father in Chapter Two, said his dad helped him keep a good perspective. His father, a lawyer, once told him: "I know you get criticized for being an only child, and people say you're spoiled and you don't know how to share, but let me tell you something. You're a very generous person and you always will be. One of the most degrading things is when those loving families come in to cut up the estate. It's human nature at its worst. I've seen feuds that will go on for years over the most minor, inconsequential thing. They're obscene. Talk about selfishness! You hear about these great, loving families that know how to share. Baloney! They can be the most selfish people in the world."

A TALE
Renée Franklin, mid-forties, trial attorney, New York City:

For me, being an only child was really wonderful in some ways. An only child gets lots of attention. You get to have more direct input. On the other hand, there are times when it's very lonely. To have a sibling or twin would have been wonderful because you'd have a buddy who would share with you the same stresses that there might be in the family. I've talked to people who have brothers and sisters who say that that probably wouldn't have happened, or say "My brother was two years older and he was mean to me." As a child, I thought it would be wonderful to have a sibling who would share my secrets, my relationship with my mom and dad, and share the living experience of growing up in a particular household. No one knows exactly what it's like except someone who's there, too. If you're an only child, there's no one with whom to relive your childhood.

I had close friends as I was growing up in L.A. I saw them on a fairly regular basis. My mother was very protective. I think she was anxious to hold on to me and not let me go, where now I am willing to try and encourage my daughter to be with other people. I experienced some aspects of a repressive mother that kept me from being as active as I might have been for fear of hurting myself. I learned to ride a bicycle at thirty-four. I started playing tennis in law school. In that sense, I'm still working at overcoming the handicaps of being an only child.

The two things that I felt cut off from, in retrospect, were the sports activity—my mother would say, "If you can't hit a ball, you don't have to try"—and the socialization. But with the socialization, it cuts two ways. I've always been an independent person, and I've cherished my freedom and independence and my own view of the world. That's something no one can take away from me. On the other hand, it sometimes makes peer-group interaction more difficult. I didn't find it as easy to be popular as someone else might have. That may also have been a function of being relatively bright in a predominantly working-class neighborhood. I did have friends who from the very beginning were tracked for college programs, even though the majority of kids in my grade school were not going to go on to college. Being tracked into special classes and not being gregarious, I was never really comfortable at junior high school dances, although now I realize that probably no one is comfortable at junior high school dances. If you have an older brother or sister who's already been through it, you may feel a little better about it.

I loved school. I loved studying. In retrospect, I was probably more social and not as shy and introverted and retiring as I thought at the time. I always had a group of four or five close friends. They were good buddies and we hung out together. I was in Campfire Girls and had a lot of really positive experiences that replaced having brothers and sisters. Perhaps it was a better way, without the sibling rivalry or the antagonism that can happen in a family. In retrospect, I suppose I had the best of both worlds. I just didn't know it at the time. At the time—I was born in 1944—there were fewer only children. Most of the people I knew had brothers and sisters, or so it seemed. It was a unique experience. So it was singular, as in the number of children in the family and also singular in the experience. I was different in a lot of ways. I was at the top of my class intellectually. I was raised by older parents in a society where parents were ten or twelve years younger. All of the onliness got underscored for me by the social experience. At the time, it felt isolating.

In some ways being an only child underscored the absence of family for me and the need to have a family. I delighted in family holidays. We always had a small family: grandma, grandpa, one aunt, two cousins, the aunt's husband and then my parents and myself. I remember those family times with a lot of joy and happiness. I now have one child and am delighted with her. I had some misgivings in terms of having just one child, although I think practically speaking, in our current society having one child is economically more feasible. And in terms of being a single parent, it is practically more feasible. I had some misgivings about not having a sibling for my daughter because I've perpetuated the kind of only-child situation I grew up in. On the other hand, I know what worked and what didn't about it.

One of the major things I've done, partially in response to that, is to have my child in a day-care situation with two very lovely, motherly women who have raised their children together and who now take in three or four children. And three of those children have formed a play group that has really grown up together, almost like siblings. They have the same two "mothers" during the day, so they share a lot of the same experiences. Since they're close to the same age, they can really share those experiences in their friendship. Thus far, my daughter seems very well socialized and able to meet new children easily and able to express herself well in new environments. I think having been with other children a lot of the time has been very good for her.

I always looked for the ideal marriage and hoped to have a child within it. But I wonder to what extent my only-childness is so deeply ingrained in me that I separate out, even to the point of being single to have a child. There are other factors, of course. I was married, divorced, lived with someone for seven years, left him. Going through the sixties, the Vietnam War, the women's movement, the seventies, I've always been a very independent person who pursued my career first. I feel like I've evolved to the point where it was a natural social evolution for me to have a child by myself in a society where it is accepted as an option that wasn't there—or was viewed negatively—before. Although I now have a child and in many ways feel the need to have a relationship with a man, I don't feel the need as strongly as a lot of people do. I'm content with a two-unit family. There are a lot of broken marriages, so there are a lot of kids raised by a single parent, anyway. Although I would still like to have my "ideal marriage," it's better to have a single-parent family by choice than to have one as the result of a marital break-up.

five

ALONE (BUT NOT NECESSARILY LONELY)

*O*ne *of the few times I have a distinct recollection of being lonely was an autumn Saturday afternoon. My uncle and I were out in the garden, pulling up the remains of the season's bounty. There were still gourds and butternut squash ripening on the vine, but the cornstalks were barren and only a few beans dangled from the poles. My neighborhood friends had gone off for the day. "When you were a kid, were you ever left without anyone to play with?" I asked my uncle. He, too, had grown up in a household as an only child, although he had older step-siblings. "Sure," he replied. "There were lots of times when there were no other kids around."*

"So what did you do?" I whined.

"Oh, I'd go to the Oval and hang around, hoping someone would show up. Or I'd do chores," he said, pointing me in the direction of a rake.

My solution, most of the time, though, was to read. I went to the Lane

School, a wooden schoolhouse that was one hundred years old. It had a room on the second floor that was alternately used as a cafeteria, gymnasium, and library. If we were having gym that day, we'd take the mats that were piled in a corner of the room and spread them on the floor so that we could do our sit-ups and tumbling. At lunchtime, a little van would roll into the schoolyard with steam tables for our hot lunches. My favorite time in this room, though, was in the afternoon when the bookcases along the side of the room were unlocked. I had a number of favorite books that I would borrow a couple of times a year. And every so often, the school department would bring in new books for a month or two. When they arrived, a teacher would place them upright on a long wooden table. I'd look them over, at their shapes and illustrations, as if choosing a new friend.

My taste, at least when I was in elementary school, ran toward mysteries. Judy Bolton was my favorite for a while. After I finished that series, I discovered Nancy Drew. Here was a wonderful role model. Nancy Drew was the only child of Carson Drew, a well-to-do lawyer in a midwestern town. Since Nancy's mother had died when she was a toddler, Nancy had grown up to be resourceful and responsible. Exposed as she was to her father's cases, she had developed a widely acclaimed talent for sleuthing. She was pretty, polite, precocious, and popular, and tooled around in a blue "roadster." To me, she was the personification of glamour. Her cases were dangerous enough to be exciting, but they were nothing I couldn't imagine myself doing: finding a hidden staircase or looking for clues in a jewelry box. The snooping I did, in fact, was pretty much confined to family history. (Who had my mother dated in high school? Which houses around town had my grandfather designed?)

Danger was pretty far removed from my life. When I was learning to ride a bike, my uncle would drive me to a school that was two miles away so that I could ride in an empty parking lot. The streets were narrow near my house, and they were afraid I'd be hit by a car. Everyone wanted to keep me safe from harm.

Still, I was able to create my own excitement. There was a well in the woods about a mile from my house. We kids called it Indian Well, and we'd comb the woods around it looking for Indian heads. We never found any, but we'd flee the forest imagining the warriors lurking near us in moccasined feet. Since we all watched The Man from U.N.C.L.E., *we'd devise plots and decide who would get to be Napoleon Solo and Illya Kuryakin. I would start to believe that we had to get the top-secret plans of the rocket to Washington. My heart would race. I would scream when one of the other kids ambushed me. In my fantasies, I was strong, brave, and smart. In reality, I got spooked a lot.*

Although I was never drawn to becoming an actress, I did tend to play out my own little dramas when I was alone. I never had an imaginary companion, which many kids, particularly only children, are said to adopt. But I did have plenty of imaginary conversations—with teachers, football players, movie stars. I was witty and always had the right rejoinder. Such solitary discussions run in the family. My father says, "When I want to have an intelligent conversation, I go downstairs and talk to myself." And he was one of twelve children.

I still enjoy my time alone, and I'm sure I always will. It's not that I don't like people. But when I'm alone, I feel free to imagine myself as I would like to be: charming, graceful, and brilliant. Solitude can be the source of great pleasure.

To me, it is one of the most powerful scenes ever projected onto a movie screen: Charles Foster Kane, one of the richest men in America, is dying alone in his castle, Xanadu. As he slips off to eternity, he utters one last word, "Rosebud." For the rest of the movie, a newspaperman investigates a life of epic wealth and emptiness, trying to discover who or what Rosebud was. Because Kane had no close family or friends, the newsman ends his search empty-handed. Orson Welles's 1941 movie, *Citizen Kane,* is a masterpiece about loneliness. It is based upon the life of newspaper tycoon William Randolph Hearst, an only child.

Dying alone, suffering alone, living alone: These prospects

terrify people. As Louise Bernikow puts it, in her book *Alone in America:* "Loneliness, for most people, is a great source of shame. It is denied. It is covered up. The impulse is to turn away from lonely people, who somehow threaten to draw us into deep quicksand, and to turn away from the idea of our own loneliness."

One of the most enduring myths about only children is that they are, by definition, lonely. "You hear people saying that they don't want to stop at one child because they don't want their child to be lonely," says Ann O'Sullivan, a New Hampshire teacher, herself an only child. "What a terrible reason for having a child. It's like getting two cats together to keep each other company."

Loneliness crosses all borders. It is hardly the domain of the only child. There are at least nineteen million people who live alone in America today, a whopping increase from five million or so in 1950. Who knows whether they are lonely or not? The most obviously lonely people are the elderly, who live, often in southern climes, in exile from family and old friends. But there is no shortage of lonely people of all ages. Teenagers, with and without siblings, often live in a netherworld of alienation, two steps past childhood, yet a foot short of adulthood. There are married people, misunderstood by a spouse, who yearn for a closer connection. New mothers, at home with infants, may feel isolated from the world they have known. Then, too, there are the workaholics, men and women who drive themselves through fifty- or sixty- hour work weeks to get ahead—or escape an empty home. Loneliness is a state of mind, a desire for closeness, that frequently has very little to do with being alone.

Yet from the time we are very young children, we are warned about the dangers of being left out, left to ourselves.

Cinderella is an only child at the mercy of her wicked step-mother and stepsisters. Little Red Riding Hood walks through the forest by herself, easy prey to the big, bad wolf. Sleeping Beauty is solitarily defenseless until Prince Charming saves her.

When I started to think about fictional only children, I was struck one night by the realization that an inordinate number of them are the focus of horror and suspense films. Norman Bates, the antihero of Alfred Hitchcock's *Psycho,* is one of the scariest movie characters of all time. It is his domineering mother, we are led to believe, who turns him into a murderer. And it is his isolation from society that allows him to get away with it. Oddly enough, Tony Perkins, the actor who portrays Norman, is also an only child.

More often, only children are the victims rather than perpetrators of violence. In *The Exorcist,* the devil finds Regan McNeil, an only child, easy quarry because her mother, an actress, is often away, and her father is entirely absent. In Brian de Palma's film *Carrie,* an only child, a teenaged girl, is harrassed and humiliated by her peers. Lacking the protection of siblings or friends, she must draw upon supernatural powers to protect herself. In Stanley Kubrick's *The Shining,* Danny, the only son, also has a psychic sensitivity. Alone with his mother and abusive father, he is snowed in at a haunted hotel high on a mountaintop. When Danny gets "shinings" that his father will kill him and his mother, he sends out messages for help.

Occasionally, too, the only child, alone with his or her instincts, becomes the hero. In a 1986 movie called *The Stepfather,* an only child named Stephanie Maine senses early on that her new stepfather may be a killer. The drama centers around her suspicions and her inability to share her fears with her mother, a young widow who desperately wants the new marriage to work. Resourceful and clever, Stephanie solves the mystery just in time. When Kate Miller is bludgeoned to death in an elevator in *Dressed to Kill,* her only child, a teenaged scientific genius, puts himself at risk in order to discover the murderer. In *Close Encounters of the Third Kind,* visitors from outer space abduct a child who lives alone with his mother. Innocent and unafraid, he accepts the aliens and eventually helps his terrified mother see their beauty.

Frank Beaver, a film professor at the University of Michigan, observes: "The only child in film seems to have the potential of becoming a loner, oftentimes more thoughtful and given to introspection. Just like the prodigal child, the single child can seem more intense."

Even in ordinary dramatic movies the isolation of the only child tends to heighten the drama. Part of the power of the Academy Award winner, *Kramer vs. Kramer,* comes from the fact that two parents are fighting over the custody of one child. It is especially interesting to contrast the New Zealand movie, *Smash Palace,* with an earlier American film called *Shoot the Moon,* starring Albert Finney and Diane Keaton. The plots of the movies, the disintegration of a marriage, are identical. Beaver contrasts the two films: "In *Shoot the Moon,* the four children are more formulaic. It's a serio-situation comedy. One child becomes the surrogate parent, another is the loudmouth, another is the angry one. Whereas in *Smash Palace,* there is much more poignancy. With a single child, the writers are forced to give her some degree of introspection. *Smash Palace* is about as fine a study of divorce and the impact of divorce as you can find. Part of that is due to the fact that they're working with one child."

Given such powerful images of the endangered only child, it is small wonder that people persist in believing that the only child is lonely. The loneliness they assign to the only child, however, is not the everyday, garden variety. It is more tragic and terrifying. People wonder how the only child, alone in the world, will survive a family crisis. Friendless, without siblings, the only child is imagined to be without help. As we will see later, only children are often better able to cope on their own than other children are. Being alone can make an individual strong. Yet one legendary case of an only child, so bereft of support, so extremely isolated, sticks in the minds of many.

The case centers on the early life of Gloria Vanderbilt, an only child whose tragic custody trial was splashed over the front pages of every American newspaper fifty years ago. Vanderbilt was born in 1924, the same year, ironically, as the creation of the cartoon character Little Orphan Annie, with whom she later came to identify. Little Gloria's father died when she was an infant, leaving her $2.5 million, a tremendous sum for the times. Her mother, Gloria Morgan Vanderbilt, barely twenty years old, took off with what would now be known as the jet set, leaving little Gloria with her nurse, Dodo. Little Gloria's grandmother, Naney Morgan, disapproved of her daughter's life of glamour and began to claim "Big" Gloria simultaneously neglected her child while squandering her daughter's fortune. Mrs. Morgan urged Gertrude Vanderbilt Whitney, little Gloria's paternal aunt, reputedly the world's richest woman, to fight for custody of little Gloria. So, at ten, Gloria Vanderbilt became the focus of scandal and a bitter custody battle. Little Gloria, herself, undermined her mother's efforts to retain custody, telling the judge that she was afraid of her mother. One damning piece of evidence: a letter that little Gloria had written to her grandmother Morgan, saying that her mother was "a rare bease."

Gloria Vanderbilt became a ward of the Supreme Court of

the State of New York, with Gertrude Whitney as custodian. In *Little Gloria . . . Happy At Last,* biographer Barbara Goldsmith writes: "In little Gloria's isolation, fear had replaced love. No one realized that little Gloria was fighting for her very life . . . " Gloria later admitted: "I can remember thinking I must speak very carefully because I knew I stood alone." Indeed, she ended up very much alone. Her Aunt Gertrude was distant, her beloved nurse Dodo was banished, and little Gloria grew up with servants. At her graduation from the tony Green Vale School, a newspaper headline bugled: ONLY CHAUFFEUR ATTENDS GLORIA VANDERBILT'S GRADUATION. Her life became a morality tale for Depression-era America, inspiring such movies as *The Poor Little Rich Girl,* starring Shirley Temple. Even the most down-and-out could feel richer than Gloria Vanderbilt.

As an adult, Gloria Vanderbilt admits in her autobiography, *Once Upon a Time,* that she knew, even as a child, that she was being manipulated into discrediting her mother. She reveals that her beloved nurse, Dodo, under Naney Morgan's orders, told her to write the letter calling her mother "a rare bease" and that she cried while doing so. Vanderbilt betrayed a distant mother out of fear of being separated from her nurse and grandmother, the only people who had eased her loneliness. She explains: "What did it matter that I didn't know the details of the plan or the nature of the plan? What I did know was that if I went along with it, Dodo Elephant and Naney Morgan would not be sent away. We three would stay together. For without them how could I live?"

Gloria Vanderbilt's story is a worst-case scenario of an isolated child being used as a pawn by unscrupulous adults. Had she had a sibling close in age (Gloria actually did have a half-sister, much older, whom she did not meet until she was a teenager), Gloria might not have been driven to such desperation. She might have had an ally.

To a great extent, Vanderbilt's extraordinary plight revolved around a fight over an extraordinarily large sum of money. Yet there are other types of family troubles that can be dangerously isolating for an only child—and leave lasting scars. Katherine, who wishes to remain anonymous, talks about growing up with parents who were actors and alcoholics, both. Now in her early twenties, Katherine is going to college and trying to shape her life. "I've always had a fear of abandonment," says Katherine. "It comes from being an only child and from being surrounded by alcoholism. You can't trust that anyone's going to be there. So much of the disease is denial. I didn't have anybody to go to for help. It was me against Mom and Dad."

Katherine says that the family was pretty poor for the first twelve years, until her mother landed a major role in a movie that turned out to be a box-office hit. "I went to quite a few different schools," she explains. "I had a very great sense of being different. Being an only child was mixed in with alcoholism. I was scared about my family. There'd be a lot of love, then the floor would fall through. Even at three, I had this feeling of, you go your way and I'll go mine. I had a sense of me against the world. I had a real sense of who I was. But my parents were so much out of it, they weren't really interested in who I was."

By the time she was a teenager, Katherine was looking for other sources of support. "Things were crazy," Katherine recalls. "I wanted some structure, some safety. I won a scholarship to the Joffrey. I joined the Catholic Church. I joined the Legion of Mary and went to old-age homes and hospitals. It was the only place I could get approval. Now I had God, ballet, and Mom and Dad. I was going to be a ballerina. I had a spiritual life and a career." Eventually, Katherine helped her parents by going with them to Alcoholics Anonymous meetings.

Today, Katherine admits that she does not want to be alone. "My parents didn't have a sense of family," she says. "We were three individuals who loved each other, but we weren't a family. Now I'm going out with a man who's one of seven children. I love spending Thanksgiving, Christmas, New Year's with them. But I can stand it for only a day. I've always been very attracted to the idea of family. I've always searched for a gang, a group of kids. I'm attracted to closeness, to living with people. That's how people belong."

Webster's points out, and Katherine would no doubt agree, that loneliness is a state of cheerless solitude. There are, of course, only children who complain about too much time alone and a feeling of estrangement. The lonely onlies, however, tend to be people who have lived amid family turmoil or in some sort of isolation. Most only children seem to treasure time they spend by themselves, a happy solitude.

Indeed, there is much to be said for spending time alone. In his book *Solitude: A Return to the Self,* British psychotherapist Anthony Storr examines the benefits of being alone. Contemporary society, he points out, emphasizes personal relationships as the source of happiness at the expense of self-knowledge. He writes: "The capacity to be alone becomes linked with self-discovery and self-realization; with becoming aware of one's deepest needs, feelings, and impulses. . . . If it is considered desirable to foster the growth of the child's imaginative capacity, we should ensure that our children, when they are old enough to enjoy it, are given time and opportunity for solitude."

Many only children get that time easily. "You wake up in

the morning and you're all alone and there's nobody to play with," recalls Flip Spiceland, the meteorologist for CNN. "You make up games, you make up imaginary friends. You spend a lot of time alone out of necessity. Instead of talking to someone, you talk to yourself and think about things. That's why I'd say I'm a more introspective person and have a much wider imagination."

The only child can become adept at entertaining himself. William M. Kelly, Jr., the retired publisher of *Money* magazine, says: "I fantasized about a lot of things. I was always by myself. I remember being a Texas Ranger. I'd lay in wait forever for robbers. I'd hide in the bushes. I don't think there was anything different about me. But I do remember that I was able to amuse myself. I don't know that I've ever been lonely. I don't dodge people. I don't like my kids to be away too long. But when I'm alone I don't feel awkward or unhappy."

Merritt Carey, the college student profiled in Chapter Two, says that being an only child was good for her because she learned what to do with herself in the afternoons after school. "I've always had to find things to do," she says. "I've spent hours on the beach just crabbing or walking. Or I'd go out in my boat. A lot of people I know just hate being with themselves, and I really cherish the time I get."

Because they tend to spend time by themselves, only children may actually develop a need to be alone. "I have an above-average need for privacy," says Christine McManus, the Tulane sophomore quoted earlier. "I have a very small circle of friends. I like to be by myself a lot. Sometimes I just want to come home and turn on the TV and be alone. If it's a loud night on the hall, I just get tired of seeing people and talking to them, tired of the constant traffic."

Marjorie Irwin, the retired teacher from Michigan, says

that she used to get up at four-thirty in the morning when she was raising her two children. "I simply had to be by myself to get my thoughts collected," she explains. "I did seek solitude. And I suppose that comes from always having the solitude with me, even though I wasn't aware of it, when I was young." Irwin believes that only children may like themselves better than the average person: "They're accustomed to finding resources in themselves. They like themselves, and that's why they don't mind being by themselves. A lot of children who have big families need the other people before they feel they can do anything. I guess they feel they need the feedback or maybe approval."

Some only children go to extraordinary lengths to spend time by themselves. Marni Weil, who is the mother of an only child in New York City, will stay up late at night just to have time to herself. "I have a craving to be alone," she says. "I stay up every night to itsy bitsy hours just so that I can be alone. It's survival. I don't care if I get three or four hours of sleep, I'm up until two or three in the morning so that I can be alone. My life is jumping from one situation to the next. I work, I come home, and everybody's got to be fed, Frederick's got to be put to bed, then everyone goes to sleep. Finally, I have a few hours in which I can read, stare at the ceiling, watch television. It's time for me. About four days a year, when I'm really exhausted, I'll fall asleep around midnight. Otherwise, I have to take the time."

What does the time alone provide for the only child? It is a chance to think, to recharge emotional batteries. It is a time to stretch out intellectually. When only children talk about enjoying solitude it does not mean that they don't enjoy the company of other people. Petra Clayton, an insurance claims adjustor in California, explains: "Being with other people can be exhilarating because I can share things. But it can also be distracting because there can be disharmony in a group. That very much gets to me. With yourself, you're pretty much in harmony."

Being alone and developing an imagination seem to go together. Only children certainly have no monopoly on fantasizing, but they do seem to have rich and varied fantasy lives. Left to their own devices, they invent friends and games. Alone in their rooms, they read books. Samantha Drab, who grew up in England after World War II and now lives in New Jersey, believes that being able to develop her imagination was one of the chief advantages of being an only child. "Although I always knew the difference between reality and nonreality, I could switch in and out easily," she recalls. "I didn't have to depend on being forced into playing what brothers and sisters would have wanted to play. They might have wanted to watch television all the time, and so I would have had nothing in my head but Superman, Batman, and Spiderman." Drab used to pretend, variously, to be an escaped prisoner from the Isle of Wight, a commando, a member of the French Resistance, or a secret agent. "They were all individuals who would have to work on their own," she observes. "I *never* had any desire to pretend to be a member of a dance troupe, a circus act, or any other group." Drab, who claims psychic ability, now works with her husband on parapsychology research. She adds: "I always liked to intrigue people."

Solitude can bestow great opportunities for creativity. Novelist John Updike observes: "I was one of the lucky only children; my sense of self-importance and ability to amuse myself has paid off." It is not surprising that many writers are only children: Robert Louis Stevenson, Hans Christian Andersen, Ann Beattie, Edward Albee, Christopher Durang,

Walter Lippmann, James Michener, Anthony Burgess, Lillian Hellman, and Iris Murdoch, to name a few.

"One of the reasons for the rarity of great imaginative
works is that in very few cases is this capacity for musing
solitude combined with that of observing mankind," wrote
Walter Bagehot, a prolific nineteenth-century English
writer. Only children may be especially suited to combining
observation with "musing solitude."

Ann Beattie, an only child, has written a number of novels
and stories that revolve around family relationships. Why?
"I suppose I didn't know exactly what families were like, so
it was more of a mystery to me," she explains. "Also by
point of fact, I was living outside of Westport, Connecticut,
and I used to ride the commuter train all the time into New
York City. I'd look at these kids on the train right there
under my nose. And while I never thought they would be
my material, or even that there was much there to explore,
I think that two years of constant exposure to them really
made me aware of them and also raised that question of
what on earth is this?

"I didn't feel lonely as a child," adds Beattie. "I think I
turned to books and things that were available to me because the family didn't ski. Books almost became logical.
Why I went on to write them is a different question, but in
some ways I think you fall into things. If you find that they
are pleasing enough, you stick with those."

Beattie claims she was no more fanciful than the average
bright child. And she is self-deprecating about her motives
as a writer. "An accurate assessment is that I had no other
skills," she explains. "To tell the truth, I never thought of
it as a career. I was attempting to feign being an academic
because the only thing I knew I didn't want in my life was
a nine-to-five job. I would have done anything, including

living off thirty-five hundred dollars a year and being vastly exploited as a teaching assistant, before I'd do that. For five years I was a teaching assistant at the University of Connecticut, where I went through the Ph.D. program and never wrote the dissertation. There were not many things at my disposal. I was sort of in exile. Coincidentally, I did start to write during those years as a hobby."

Fantasizing can be valuable to anyone, not just novelists. Baron Bates, the businessman quoted in Chapter Three, remembers spending hours in the woods behind his home pretending to be a cowboy. "Fantasy played a big role for me," he says. One dividend has been a lifetime of enjoyment of amateur acting. But Bates believes that the ability to fantasize has also been very helpful to his career as an automobile executive. "If I don't want to dwell on current problems, I think about what I'm going to do one and two years from now," Bates explains. "I probably spend more time than I should thinking about something like that. I'm sure it's a mature form of fantasizing. There is a certain advantage to that. If you're able to project ahead it can be said that you are running away from reality. But you can also be said to be visionary."

Of course, people can take fantasizing too far. Barbara Polk, a music teacher who grew up in a small Wisconsin town with her mother, father, and grandmother, used fantasy to withdraw from the constant attention. "I retreated into a fantasy world a lot," she remembers. "I learned early, living with those three adults, to pull off into my own little world. That was a comfortable, safe place to be. I would spend two or three hours in an afternoon just sitting, totally lost in fantasy." She used to dream about being part of a larger family, or of helping out her aunt, who had six sons.

When she was in her thirties, married and the mother of three children, she developed an addiction to Valium, which had been prescribed to her by a doctor because she was having trouble sleeping. "It was an accident," she recalls. "I loved what Valium did for me. For one thing, it made me sleep, which was nice. Valium helped me to retreat into a world again where I sort of floated. When I was really into the drug, I used to spend afternoons just lying on the bed with images floating through my mind, back in that fantasy world that was familiar from childhood." Drug-free for over five years, Polk now takes bicycle trips to find solitude.

When loneliness strikes—as it does strike everyone— many only children feel they cope better than some of their friends. Joe and Robin Bruna, two only children married to each other, admit that as they have grown older they have become "very alone in the world." They do have one daughter who lives not far from them in Kentucky. Yet they do not spend a lot of time with her and her husband. For the Brunas, being alone is not a problem. "One important aspect of being an only child is that you have to learn how to play and amuse yourself as a little child," says Robin. "I think it's something that holds you in good stead in your old age. I can stay home alone here and have quite a good time. I can read, I can putter around, I can do more darn things. And Joe has all kinds of hobbies." Robin does not feel as if she needs to be around people. "I'm not saying I don't like to be around them," she quickly adds. "I'd like to be around people maybe more than I am. I'm just not devastated by it the way some people are who are used to having a household. The ones who are used to everyone coming in and out like Grand Central Station will say they can't stand being alone. They'll tell me they have to turn on the radio or the TV to have some noise. I say, what for? I don't need to make noise. I have my own thoughts. I think that is part of being an only child that makes us different, and I still think it's an asset."

Being alone and living alone does not seem to hold the terror for only children that it holds for others. "I suppose I could have been bored and frustrated as an only child had I had a different family," says Ann Beattie, "but I knew the individuals around me loved me and wished me to be happy. In some ways, I've never minded my own company. When I did get divorced many years ago, people would say to me, 'Wait until you see the horrors of living alone.' Well, I never did. I've always had to rely on my own company. I did even as a child because my parents didn't jump around and play Clarabell with me every minute. I think that actually was an advantage, at least for me. I like privacy. I don't get paranoid if the phone doesn't ring or people aren't around. I just think: 'Oh, great. This gets to be privacy. I know what that is.' That's actually been something that helped me personally, to be able to stand myself. I think a lot of people who are used to being entertained and noticed early on expect that to carry over into adulthood. I didn't expect that at all. So, it's been very helpful, especially in such a lonely career as being a writer. This may sound corny to say, but I can't imagine a situation in which I couldn't function. I don't think I'm tied to anything. I have bonds with people. But the sad notion is that I do think everybody is alone."

A TALE
Margot Adler, early forties, reporter for National Public Radio, New York City:

I was very much a wanted child. I was born premature, at seven months, and almost died. My mother was thirty-nine and had tried to have other children, but she had had two or three miscarriages. I come from a family with very few relatives. I am not only an only child, but my father had three sisters, none of whom had kids. So I'm the last of that entire family.

This may have nothing to do with being an only child—or maybe it does—but my two earliest recollections of all time involve no other people. They are sort of utopian. In one of them, I'm one and a half, and we still live on Croton-on-Hudson. I'm walking up a staircase, just barely walking, and they're big steps. There are roses all around and it's entirely beautiful. The other memory is very similar. I'm running out onto a lawn, and I'm chasing a butterfly. Again, it's absolutely gorgeous. But again, there are no people.

Actually, relatives said that I didn't talk until fairly late, as if I didn't need to. They explained it by saying that everything was given to me, so I didn't need to talk. But the way I would explain it is that I was always basically content to be alone doing nothing. I've always been able to be alone and not really need other people to make my world real.

I had, and still have, an incredibly rich fantasy life. In my youth, I spent hours a day in fantasy. Almost all the fantasies were of a fictional, somewhat historical, or science-fictional nature. I would be an Egyptian slave, or a telepathic secret agent, or a Quaker being persecuted in the seventeenth century. Starting at seven, I would get these characters from books. I would walk into books and live them out. I'm sure that being an only child had some influence on that since I spent so much of my time alone. I've never reconciled in my mind whether they were a waste of time or part of a creative process.

In all of them, I was essentially trying to make friends. But the characters were all different and persecuted, like a Quaker who struggles to find acceptance in a hostile world. Every single one of these fantasies had that theme: the alien. I've had those kind of visionary images ever since I was seven years old. I even remember the first one.

I was taken to Europe when I was four and a half. I was too young to go to Europe, because I didn't know any foreign language. I remember I was taken to a camp for Austrian children for a couple of days. I was given a dirndl to wear, and when I came home I wore this Austrian dirndl for a number of years. I had this fantasy of being a child going to school and knowing no English: walking through the halls and being somewhat distant, being alien. That's the first fantasy I remember. Every single one that followed was a much more elaborate and literary version: How do you make friends with someone if you feel you are internally very different? I would say that throughout my life, I've always felt that I was somehow alien.

The bad side to that was that for a while I was not very popular. When my parents began to have marital problems—they divorced when I was thirteen—things drastically changed. Amazing things happened. My mother was hospitalized when she tried to commit suicide. I was suddenly brought up by my father for a few months and then again

by my mother. Interestingly enough, that coin-
cided with a time when I suddenly began making
peace at school, when I suddenly started becoming
popular. I became the peacemaker in my family,
trying to get my parents to agree, which they
didn't. And I tried to be a peacemaker at school.
So, suddenly I was valued, suddenly I had friends.
Still, high school was an unmitigated disaster. It
was a combination of my parents' divorce and
having gone to a small progressive school and then
being thrown into a large public high school
where I was completely over my head. I gained an
enormous amount of weight and sat home.

Some of the best things and some of the worst
things about my life were due to being an only
child. I think the worst was that it was very hard
for me to learn to be a social being. Of course, it's
hard for me to know whether that really was true
or whether I simply felt that way because I was
the grandchild of Alfred Adler. My father is an
Adlerian shrink. A big emphasis in Adlerian psychology is social interest. So one of the ways I
remember being punished was being told that I
was selfish and that I wasn't thinking of other
people. To this day, when I forget someone or am
oblivious to someone's else's needs, the worst
feelings of guilt descend upon me.

One of the most important things about being
an only child is the chance to escape role definition. My mother told me that before I was born,
before they knew if I was a boy or a girl, I was
called Pago, which was for Peter or Margot. From
the very beginning, I was basically allowed to be

everything I wanted to be. I was supposed to be everything. No one ever gave me a train set—and I wanted one—but for a while I never really felt a lot of the sexism in society. Even though my mother lived fairly traditionally, she came of age in the thirties as a bohemian. She had first married a poet-musician when she was eighteen and had run away from home. She did all kinds of crazy things. So even though she ended up as a housewife in the fifties, the household was very much the kind of place where you'd find the books of Simone de Beauvoir. My father was sympathetic to Marxism, so a certain amount of lip service was always paid to, I wouldn't call them feminist, but certainly egalitarian, ideals. I went to progressive schools until high school.

I was brought up in a very atheistic household in which I was told that my parents believed in the brotherhood of man. When I was twelve, my school studied ancient Greece for that whole year. I decided that the real religion for me was of the Greek gods and goddesses. Deep down, I wanted to be Artemis or Athena. This was back in 1958 or 1959. They were terrific role models compared to the images of women lurking around in the late fifties, anyway. Interestingly enough, they are very solo-oriented goddesses. To this day the virgin goddesses of the ancient Greek religion are my role models.

I also attribute my entry into radio as the appropriate vehicle for an only child, particularly live, free-form radio. Besides making a living as a reporter—an observer-outsider position if there ever was one—I have done a live free-form show since 1972. Sometimes I sit in the studio alone in total darkness watching the dials blinking. It feels like being in a spaceship hurtling through the galaxy. One speaks to the world, sound waves traveling through the ether, never quite knowing when you pick up the phone calls who or what will come in—or even if anyone is out there.

Now I'm forty-two and happily married and even able to have some true friends. But I often think my inner and outer lives have been irrevocably determined by being an only child.

six

INDEPENDENCE

AND

INDIVIDUALISM

A lthough I spent the first part of my life trying to fit in with others, somewhere along the line I decided that it was not just okay, but desirable, to be different. I can't remember when I began to think I was unique. I suppose it was during adolescence, a time when most kids accentuate the differences between themselves and their elders.

I came of age during the tumultuous late sixties. I went to a public school, Gloucester High School, where the boys were required to take ROTC. The official social life of the school revolved around "military" events: the officers' party, the sergeants' party, the field day, in which the boys (and the girls' drill team) marched through the city of Gloucester. As a freshman—nearsighted but too vain to wear my glasses—I would walk through the halls amid a sea of olive-green uniforms, speaking to no boy, because I couldn't distinguish one from another. Instead of looking more attractive, I looked stupid. Instead of getting dates, I got a reputation as a snob. My one attempt to be part of a uniformed group—I actually tried out for the drill team—ended in failure because I never was too quick in telling my left from my right.

By the time I was a junior, everyone seemed to be questioning everything. We protested mandatory ROTC. It was made voluntary. As editor of the school newspaper, I wrote an editorial demanding an end to dress-code rules. They fell—and hems rose. I no longer obsessed about what other kids thought of me. Even though I had finally gotten my driver's license, I began to ride my bicycle the four miles to school my senior year, boycotting both bus and the family Pontiac, to make a political statement about ecology. Instead of being loudly hooted, as I expected, I actually got a lot of compliments and a few other kids started riding bikes to save the environment.

Being different, I found, could have its rewards.

I chose to go to a women's college, even though the seventies was the time when all the Ivy League schools were going coed. While I was in high school I had watched a boy be elected class president year after year. A girl back then could not hope to win that kind of lofty post. I knew this was inherently wrong, even though I was not to acquire the vocabulary to express this idea until later. So I went off to Mount Holyoke because it was a women's college. I wanted to be free to develop without the competition stacked against me.

Even though I had been brought up in a traditional household—traditional in the respect that the man earned most of the money and the woman took care of the house—I learned that I was expected to be somebody, do something. My aunt had also given me the idea early on that I should always be able to support myself, that I should even have a career. This was a pretty progressive idea for the fifties, when most girls were steered toward marriage and motherhood. While my aunt's idea of an appropriate career focused on school teaching, mine eventually ran in another direction. When I told her that I wanted to be a journalist, she told me that that was like some kid in a school play wanting to be a Hollywood movie star.

While I was on vacation my freshman year, my father and I were driving home from Boston along Route 128. He told me in a fatherly way that he wanted me to have a "normal" life—to get married and have children. I was so irate that I almost drove into a guard rail at sixty miles per hour. I told him that I hadn't worked this hard just to be like everybody else. After that, he started telling me I'd make a great lawyer. Why not apply to law school?

But I felt journalism was my calling. What I wanted to do more than anything else was to become a writer for Time *magazine. I had no idea how hard it would be until I went to New York for my interview. The man in personnel told me that I would need the equivalent of a master's degree to even work as a reporter-researcher for the magazine and that I could not even aspire to becoming a writer until I was much older and more experienced. I was thrilled, then, when I was hired after graduation to work as a researcher at Time-Life Books. Within two years, though, I convinced the chief of research at* Time *to hire me. Although there were few women writers, I knew that I still wanted to become one. My research duties were frequently tedious, but I reported a lot of stories. Fortunately I got paired up with one of the four women writers at the magazine, and she helped me find opportunities to actually write some* Time *stories. By the time I asked for a writer's trial, I had already had six pieces published in the magazine. My nine-month trial went well. At twenty-six, I was formally anointed as a* Time *writer. My dream had not been so foolish, after all.*

At about the same time I made another leap in imagination. I had always, with good reason, thought of myself as uncoordinated and unathletic. Indeed, I had always suffered the utter humiliation of being the last person picked for school sports. My first winter in New York, I put on about five pounds. As the daffodils burst through the ground in Central Park, I started to think about how I could shed the weight. I started running because it seemed cheap and efficient. There were a few other joggers, and we pretty much knew each other by sight, if not by name. Since this was in the days before Casio watches—or women's running clothes, for that matter—I thought I'd run a race simply to find out how fast I could run. I did well and soon found myself "training" with marathoners, mostly men.

Gradually, I began to think of myself as an athlete. Only four years earlier, it had been against all rules for a woman, any woman, to run a marathon. By the time I was running, there was a small group of dedicated women athletes. In 1976, the first year that the New York City Marathon was held in the five boroughs, I was one of eighty-eight women runners. I was amazed at the primal scream I heard from women on the sidelines. "Go beat him, honey," yelled one woman with pink haircurlers, who was jumping up and down on her Brooklyn stoop. It was scary and exhilarating at the same time. Even though I was falling apart physically by the last few miles, I plastered a smile on my face. I felt I had to prove that women could do this thing. And I certainly had to prove that I could.

Although eventually there would be more women writers at Time *and many more women marathoners, I had tried something hard in which women had little, if any, track record. It was my special pride, a secret machisma, that I was accomplishing something unusual—putting in twenty-hour closing days for* Time, *sleeping twelve hours on Saturday, then going out and winning a trophy for a twenty-mile race on Sunday. Everyone, if they make the definition narrow enough, can feel unique. As a child, I had started out feeling different. As an adult, I ended up feeling special.*

Declaring one's independence from parents is the hallmark of adulthood. Some people—whether they are the only one or one of many—never successfully separate. Many parents use love, guilt, presents, even mortgage payments, to keep their children close by. Are the parents of only children more likely to hang on? Are onlies more likely to cling? The answer depends upon the temperaments and circumstances of parents and child.

Jonathan Bulkeley, the young publishing executive quoted in Chapter Four, describes his tug between dependence and independence. As the only child of two only children, he says, "I think the fact that we were all only children brought us closer together." Sometimes, though, he had trouble asserting his autonomy. "When I was looking at prep schools, they forced me to go to Hotchkiss, which was fine. I was third generation. I don't think that was a bad decision, because, how, at the age of thirteen, can you decide where you want to go to school? For college, they didn't force me. I wanted to go to Yale. I was seventh generation. There was tradition there that I wanted to continue.

"I think I'm both independent and dependent," he says. "I see my parents constantly and talk to them constantly, yet I have another side that says I know what I'm doing." While Bulkeley says that his parents did not push him in any particular career direction, they still spend a lot of time worrying about him. "Take this trip to the Amazon I'm about to go on," he says. "My mother is absolutely petrified. She's afraid I'll die in the Amazon; get bitten by a snake, fall into a river, disappear, be gone forever, catch malaria, be strung up by cannibals, you name it, it's gone through her mind. And what makes it worse is that she's in Kenya right now. So, I say to her: 'I'm more worried about you than you should be about me.'" Bulkeley concludes: "It's nice to know they care, but as you're growing up, you want some autonomy. And sometimes you don't get it. You really have to fight for it."

There is a popular misconception that the only child is a clinging vine, overly dependent on others, especially parents. Yet the opposite may be more true. In 1974, a government researcher, Kenneth W. Terhune, surveyed studies done on children and concluded that children from large families were actually more dependent on their families than only children. In another study, Sharryl Hawke and David Knox discovered that 38 percent of young only children felt that self-confidence was one of their advantages. Why? Apparently, freed from competition for parental affection and attention, the only child feels more secure.

One of the most self-confident characters in literature is Dorothy Gale of *The Wonderful Wizard of Oz.* An only child who lives with her Auntie Em and Uncle Henry in Kansas, Dorothy is picked up by a tornado and dropped in the Land of Oz. With her trusted friend and canine companion, Toto, Dorothy begins the long journey home. Even when she is in danger, she is fair and polite to every creature. She has high standards and rebukes the Cowardly Lion, for one, when he does not live up to them. When her survival depends upon it, she is capable of killing the Wicked Witch of the West. Even after she is made an honorary princess, Dorothy remains true to her values. She believes in herself.

I think that many only children, like Dorothy, believe in themselves. Being the center of attention early in life helps to foster a sense of being important. Being alone with thoughts and fantasies helps only children to know themselves.

Like Dorothy, only children seem to be responsible children. Sometimes it is out of necessity; sometimes, desire. Because her family was poor, Shirley Pettijohn, a California woman now in her fifties, took on many adult tasks when she was young. "I can remember when I was four years old, my job was to pick up the chips when my father chopped wood," she says. "As I got older I had more responsibility. I carried in the lighter logs, watered and fed the chickens. When I was nine, the war was underway, and my mother went to work in a war factory. My father was in the fields.

So I did all the cooking, all the washing, all the ironing. I made their beds every day. I took everything in this house under control, plus I took care of the chickens. I grew up knowing how to cope with situations."

Margaret Mead used to leave her daughter, Mary Catherine Bateson, with a surrogate family when she went off on her anthropological field trips. "I seemed to have felt responsible for myself a great deal," recalls Bateson. "I felt independence and autonomy. Responsibility for one's self is a form of independence. Responsibility for other people is a form of burden."

It is quite possible that only children develop a sense of self-reliance sooner and more deeply than others. When parents have only one child, especially if they are older, they may consciously foster a spirit of independence. Judy Anderson-Wright, the early-childhood educator quoted in Chapter Three, grew up with grandparents who taught her that she should be able to take care of herself. "My parents divorced when I was three," she says. "My father was in intelligence; my mother disappeared. I haven't seen or heard from her since I was five." Even after her father remarried and had other children, Anderson-Wright chose to remain with her grandparents. "I was taught to be independent," she says. "Because I had a lot of time alone at home, I was curious about investigating things. I became a very creative person in order to entertain myself. My strength as an adult comes from that quest to be creative and independent. My grandparents often told me: 'You only have you.' They articulated that a lot."

But most only children figure that out anyway. "I always grew up thinking that I had to take care of myself, that I had to be there for myself, had to achieve, that there wasn't going to be anyone to take care of me," says Renée Franklin.

"If you're part of a big family, chances are you always have a place to live, a roof over your head, and you've always got a loan to carry you through. That's something an only child doesn't have." Kathleen Meenehan, a probation counselor in juvenile court, puts it a little bit differently: "In the back of my mind, I know that I belong only to me."

Necessity can be the mother of independence. Frances, a woman in her fifties, was traumatized by her parents' divorce. "I didn't begin to question being an only child until I was in my teens and my parents got divorced," she says. "Up until then, I always felt right with the world. We had a terrifically nice life. I had a lot when I was a kid—a lot for a lower-middle-class family. I had more clothes and better-looking clothes than anyone else. I'd be dressed from Filene's Basement, so it was on the cheap, but it was wonderful quality. Then, after the divorce, I had almost nothing.

"My parents had a particularly ugly divorce," she says. "My mother left, and my father would say things like 'If you had been a better child, your mother wouldn't have left.' If you have two or three kids, that sort of thing can be diluted. So I personally felt responsible. I knew that wasn't true, but I felt I should have been able to keep them together. It was so bad that they were fighting in the corridor of the courthouse in Boston. It was practically a scene for a movie. I was crying, they were yelling, and this great guard with an Irish accent came along and said: 'Aren't you ashamed? I'm going to walk this child down the corridor, and I want you to pull yourselves together.' "

Despite the fierce custody battle, there was a time when Frances was fourteen and living alone in a Boston boarding-house because she didn't want to live with her father, and her mother had moved out of the state. Her father eventually got a court order, and Frances moved in with him and his new wife. "Because I was an only child, I was very smart and mouthy and had been encouraged to be that way," she says. But her "smart" behavior, plus some skipping of school, brought her father back to court, this time to have her declared "unmanageable." Says Frances: "Taking me to court was the best thing my family could have done, because I found a very nice social worker who urged me to get on with my life."

For a while, Frances was living in a home in Boston that was a sort of holding pen for girls who were going to be sentenced by the court as runaways. But she had a room of her own and spent a lot of time reading. In the summer, she went away to a resort to wait on tables. "Because I was an only child, I had an incredible strength regarding what I did and didn't want to do. When I got to this resort, I decided I'd quit school. So this marvelous social worker said, 'You can do that. But there's a private school in New Hampshire where you can go on a scholarship.' "

Not only did Frances finish high school, but she was accepted at Pembroke College, then the women's part of Brown University. "Brown was a good school, and it was always important to me to go to the best," she says. "The conviction that what I did was important carried me through the ten or fifteen years after my parents divorced, which were brutal years."

There is a less obvious type of independence that one sometimes perceives when talking to only children. They often seem to be independent or unconventional thinkers. Again, there are good reasons for this. Many only children talk about the singularity of their experience. At worst, that uniqueness can make an only child feel different in a way that is troublesome. At best, it can make the only child feel special. Many only children realize that they are different from other children, at least regarding their upbringing. The crucial issue seems to be whether being "different" has positive or negative connotations.

The idea of being different is most poignant when it is connected with being rejected, being an outcast. Pearl, the only child of Hester Prynne in Nathaniel Hawthorne's *The Scarlet Letter,* personifies her mother's sin of passion. Exiled into the woods, Hester lives an ascetic life of good works while indulging Pearl with magnificent garments. Pearl is a wild but wise child. Hawthorne wrote: "The child could not be made amenable to rules. In giving her existence, a great law had been broken; and the result was a being whose elements were perhaps beautiful and brilliant, but all in disorder; or with an order peculiar to themselves. . . ." As Pearl grew up, she retaliated against the taunting children and instinctively rejected the Reverend Arthur Dimmsdale, her unacknowledged father. "In the little chaos of Pearl's character there might be seen emerging—and could have been, from the very first—the steadfast principles of an un-flinching courage,—and uncontrollable will,—a sturdy pride, which might be disciplined into self-respect,—and a bitter scorn of many things, which, when examined, might be found to have the taint of falsehood in them."

Pearl was an outcast to an extreme degree. But the role of outsider is not unfamiliar to many only children. Bonnie Ernst, an aerobics instructor in Seattle, always felt at odds with others. "My being an only child was noted a lot at the time," she recalls, "because it was a bizarre thing in the fifties. Everybody in my class was one of two or three. Teachers related to them better, because they knew their brothers and sisters. I didn't have that connection. At school

I felt I was on the outside. At family gatherings I felt that I was on the outside. I was the one who my cousins would beat up on." Even today, Ernst feels an uncomfortable lack of connection. "People come and go," she sighs. "I don't have the feeling that I'll ever have a family. The background isn't there for having a complete one."

For some only children, like Ernst, the sense of being different is damaging. Yet for others, like Hawthorne's Pearl, being different can eventually strengthen character. Renée Franklin often felt troubled being an only child when she was young. "Yet I saw being different as being special, even at my most insecure times," she says. "I still see it as special. I will always have some of those problems of being free, independent, and special. But there are things I see as a plus that I would never let go of. There is something that being an only child gives to you. You get the sense that you're wonderful and special, and you can carry that with you. Having an only child myself, I certainly think of her as wonderful and special and unique. Certainly, all people are, and I would seek to do that with all children if I had more than one—yet somehow I wonder if that would get lost along the way with more children."

Feeling special can increase a person's sense of self-confidence. It is most helpful when it is an inner conviction that is not obvious to others. Laura Stein-Stapleford says: "When there's only one, you are told time and time again that you're very special. And you start to think you're very special. That doesn't sit well with your peers. I think feeling special, though, made me much more motivated. I really don't think about failure very often. I think I can do almost anything I set my mind to. I don't impose many limits on myself. There may be a situation where I get a piece of work, and I don't know much about it. But I have an innate sense of confidence that somehow I'm going to pull it off."

Dorothy, a homemaker in Michigan who has four adult children, talks about how the sense of being special has sustained her throughout her life. Her father died when she was seven. Soon afterward, her mother put her on a bus to go to boarding school. As they parted, Dorothy's mother told her: "Dorothy, you're very special. Just hold your shoulders back and you can do anything you want to do." Fifty years later, when Dorothy was having a hip operation, the doctors and nurses at the hospital were amazed to see how well she was recovering. Dorothy says: "As I sat in bed, I thought, 'Thank you, Mother.' The idea of being special has helped me through many crises and tragedies."

Only children also seem to be less bound by the conventions of traditional sex roles. It is striking how many girls, especially, grow up with aspirations that are both masculine and feminine. The reason is not hard to understand: The only child must fulfill the expectations of both mother and father. Because of this, many only girls get the best of both worlds.

In less enlightened times, only children raised some concern because they seemed to be more flexible about gender roles than people who had come from larger families organized along traditional mother/housewife and father/breadwinner roles. Researchers noticed that female only children sometimes exhibited traits usually associated with boys; male only children sometimes exhibited "feminine" characteristics.

In 1984, psychologists Phyllis A. Katz and Sally L. Boswell decided to compare the gender roles in the one-child family with those in larger families. The families selected fell along fairly traditional lines, with the fathers providing more or most of the family income and mothers staying home with young children or working part-time. Despite the traditional division of labor, though, researchers found that families with one child tended to be more politically liberal.

Concern about gender seems to be less important to parents of only children than to parents of more than one. This would stand to reason, since people who have strong feelings about replicating themselves will usually have at least two children to get a good shot at both a girl and a boy. Yet, in testing parental reactions to cross-sex play, such as boys playing with dolls, Katz and Boswell found that fathers of only-child boys were less tolerant than fathers of boys with siblings. On the other hand, fathers of one girl were more tolerant of cross-sex behavior in their daughters. While fathers might want their daughters to emulate them, there seems to be a real aversion to boys being made "sissies." Mothers of one child, on the other hand, were more relaxed about both sexes. The result: Only-born girls were less tied to gender roles than male onlies, who in some respects were more traditional than boys with siblings.

Katz and Boswell found that all parents were equally unenthusiastic about a son going into a traditionally female occupation, such as secretarial work. But parents, especially mothers, were very positive about the idea of their daughters going into male-oriented jobs and professions. It is possible that the parents of only children tend to value pursuits commonly considered masculine and encourage their only child to engage in these. The researchers concluded: "The most tolerant parents were those with an only daughter."

"I used to think that the worst thing that could happen to a female was to have a brother, in the sense of getting the message of who matters," says anthropologist Mary Cather-

ine Bateson. "The preference for the male would get incul-
cated so early in a mixed family. Whereas a lot of the most
enterprising women are women whose fathers accepted
them as a partial substitute for the boys they didn't have. I
have one friend who's one of three sisters, and they're all
M.D.s. If they had had one male in that family, I bet none
of those women would be doctors now."

"When I was a child, I wished I was a boy," says Samantha Drab. Growing up in England, she found that the opportunities boys had were much more exciting. "Girls were so
dull," she recalls. "They did embroidery and had to do what
their mothers told them. I was a tomboy. I was adventurous.
I spent hours sitting by my father while he repaired his
motorbike. I used to get high on the smell of oil. I wanted
to know how things worked and why they worked."

Female only children I talked to often pointed to their
fathers as a source of self-confidence. "My father taught me
that if there was anything I couldn't do, it was because I
personally could not do it or I couldn't allow myself to do
it," recalls one woman. "It was not because I was a girl. It
isn't that my father ever encouraged me to be a boy—which
is kind of funny, since my middle name was Anthony. My
mother was more ridden with fears. She's changed over the
years. She had a pretty fifties outlook." Petra Clayton, a
California insurance adjustor who grew up in Germany just
after World War II, says: "I was a boy and girl rolled up in
one ball because the hopes of my parents centered on me.
I would attribute my more liberated heart to the fact that
they wanted to see me succeed in both worlds. I wanted to
grow up and be self-sufficient."

"My mother gave me enough of a sense of what women
hadn't been able to do," recalls Texan Elizabeth Clark. "My
daddy saw the things you could do. Here's the best advice

they ever gave me: My daddy said you can do anything you want to, you just have to believe in yourself. My mother said you can do anything you want, but it pays to be a lady." Clark's father owns his own private investigation business. "When I was growing up," she says, "we were always going to be Clark & Clark, Attorney and Investigations. I don't know, maybe we will someday."

Roles seem to be less standardized in a lot of one-child households. Student Christine McManus says that she and her father are very close. "When I was little we'd do simple things together: go grocery shopping, ride through the car wash with the big brushes, go to the movies once a week. Now we don't do as much together, but we still talk. We'll sit and watch TV football together."

Ann O'Sullivan, a teacher in her forties who is planning to apply to medical school, believes that being an only child was a "really positive thing." As a young adult, she became involved in the women's movement and joined a conscious-ness-raising group. "I realized that I didn't go through the same type of thing in my family that other people did, because there weren't any roles in my family," she says. "I mean, I did everything." Her father, a lawyer, had grown up in a wealthy household with servants until the Depression. "When I was about seven or eight, I learned how to jack up the house and put in the beams. And my mother taught me how. My father was good at being a lawyer, but he didn't know how to do any of those typically masculine things. But my mother enjoyed them. I grew up thinking it was odd that my next-door neighbor's mother ironed. My father did the ironing. He liked it."

As more options in life open up for both men and women, male only children may be more willing to try untraditional roles. Two well-known only children, the late John Lennon and ABC newsman Ted Koppel, both took time out from their public lives to raise children.

It may be that the less traditional upbringing of the only child makes him or her more comfortable with individuality. An only child must find his own path, after all, not follow in advance of or behind a sibling. Emancipated to some degree from tradition and authority, the only child may personify the personal independence that is at the core of American democracy.

There are only children, real and imagined, who symbolize the American ideal of originality. Charles Lindbergh, the son of a Congressman from Minnesota and his estranged wife, became the hero of the 1920s after he flew his Spirit of St. Louis solo across the Atlantic. Superman, at fifty, can still change the course of mighty rivers, bend steel with his bare hands, and fight for truth, justice, and the American way. And what is more all-American than Huckleberry Finn, floating down the Mississippi, searching for adventure?

The heroic loner is a literary tradition. Hamlet must seek truth and wisdom after Claudius kills his father and marries his mother. Homer's Ulysses, in both the *Odyssey* and the *Iliad,* is close to no one, except for his father and son. In analyzing the character of Ulysses, Harvard psychiatrist Bennett Simon asks: "Is the 'only child' fantasy in some way related to the birth of a certain kind of individualism that may be the hallmark of Western civilization?"

In *Solitude: A Return to the Self,* British psychiatrist Anthony Storr writes: "It may be the case that, the less a person feels himself to be embedded in a family and social nexus, the more he feels that he has to make his mark in individual fashion. . . . Originality implies being bold enough to go

beyond accepted norms. . . . Those who are not too dependent upon, or too closely involved with, others, find it easier
to ignore convention."

When you talk to only children, you get the sense that
they may indeed be less afraid of living outside the rules.
Renée Franklin feels comfortable marching to her own
drum. "I've never conformed," she says. "At least in the
sense of taking life's steps at the expected time or in the
conventional way. Instead, I've made decisions based on
what is right for me at a given time. I married in high school,
divorced when everyone else was marrying. I lived with a
man before it was socially acceptable. Ultimately, I had a
child on my own. During the late sixties, I was a self-styled
liberal—which my relatives labeled 'hippie'—marching
against the war, while refusing to conform to movement
politics or hippie dress codes as well as the established main-
stream.

"When I finally went to law school, I went at night, after
attempts at a New York acting career and a boutique clothing business. I think I chose trial work because it integrated
the unique elements of my background. My friends—artists,
actors, policemen from law school—all thought I'd become
a defense attorney. To their surprise, I became a prosecutor.
I prosecute because I love what I'm doing and believe in our
government and the laws I enforce. However, there's an
irony to my having become an enforcer of society's rules.
And, in many ways, I've never felt entirely in sync with
other prosecutors. My closest friends are still in creative-arts
fields or therapists or defense attorneys. I keep trying to
balance who I am with what I've chosen to become. I am still
working on carving myself a niche and molding myself to
fit it. As I raise a child and grow older, more of what I want
from the process seems to be more conventional and very

like what everyone else wants. Being out of step with the rest of society is a position in which I've always been comfortable, but I may be coming full circle to find that I want to be in step."

Freed from the confinements of traditional roles and a large family, many only children are not just "free to be me." They are also free to reinvent themselves as they get older. Only children are constantly thrown onto their own resources. Many go through a continual evolution, a sort of revision.

A classic example from fiction is F. Scott Fitzgerald's Jay Gatsby. Apparently alone in the world, Gatsby invents a dazzling persona. He tells Nick Carroway that he is "the son of some wealthy people in the Middle West—all dead now." He is a celebrated party-giver, a man of notoriety, suspected of many things. As it turns out, though, Gatsby was born James Gatz in North Dakota. His parents were "shiftless and unsuccessful farm people." Fitzgerald wrote: "His imagination never really accepted them as his parents at all. The truth was that Jay Gatsby of West Egg, Long Island, sprang from his Platonic conception of himself. He was a son of God . . ."

Gatsbyesque reinvention happens not just in fiction. Movie star Clark Gable underwent a similar self-creation. William C. Gable was born in 1901 in a small Pennsylvania town. Less than a year later, his mother, Addie Gable, died, and her baby boy went to live with grandparents. Even though his father remarried a woman who was devoted to the young boy, Gable eventually severed his roots. "Clark Gable always considered himself a man without a family," wrote biographer Lyn Tornabene in *Long Live the King.* "He had no happy memories of his past; therefore he had no past at all. To all intents and purposes, Clark Gable the movie star sprang full-grown from a film projector."

It is hard to know who created Marilyn Monroe. The world's most enduring sex symbol, Monroe is another only child who became a lifetime fugitive from a troubled past. Although she was born Norma Jean Mortenson in 1926, it was never clear who her real father was. Her mother, a film cutter in the movie industry, was unable to care for her. Norma Jean moved from one foster home to another and spent two years in the Los Angeles Orphans' Home. She married at sixteen so that she would not have to return to the orphanage.

As she worked her way up through the studio system, she became a big star, an American Venus. Yet, she was constantly trying to improve herself, taking acting lessons with Lee Strasberg long after she was famous. She married baseball great Joe DiMaggio, divorced him, then married playwright Arthur Miller. There is widespread speculation that she had an affair with President John F. Kennedy. She struggled all her life to refine and improve herself, finally dying, an apparent suicide and an unfinished woman.

Archie Leach was another only child who tried to escape an unhappy life, this one in Bristol, England. His father drank too much, his mother was committed to an insane asylum when her son was nine. At thirteen, Archie left home to join a group of teenage acrobats and by seventeen was a stilt walker on Coney Island. Eventually he landed acting roles on Broadway. When Paramount signed him to a five-year contract in 1932, he changed his name to Cary Grant.

Fortunately for him, he was more successful at life than Marilyn Monroe. Archie turned himself, with the help of Hollywood, into the debonair man who symbolized sex and class to millions of people. Grant once told an interviewer: "I pretended to be a certain kind of man onscreen. I patterned myself on a combination of [British music-hall star]

Jack Buchanan, Noël Coward, and Rex Harrison, and I became that man in life. I became me. Or he became me. Or
we met at some point." At sixty-five he stopped making
movies to become a full-time father to his newly born
daughter, his only child.

A TALE
James E. Reynolds, early thirties, reporter for Sports
Illustrated, *New York City:*

I think that much of my comfort in being an
only child comes from being part of an interracial
family. You're pretty much isolated and alienated
from society. Being an only child isn't dissimilar
to that. You're an island unto yourself. My parents have never felt a strong need to belong to
anything. They're not bridge players or country
clubbers. They're not group people at all. They've
learned to be very happy within their own world.
I was brought up almost in a perfect environment
to nurture an only child in terms of independence.
I give them a lot of credit now.

My father was probably one of the few educated blacks when he was living in Georgia. He's
an only child also. He was born in 1913 and graduated from Morehouse. My father was in the
theatre. He was a singer and actor who played in
Porgy and Bess in the 1950s. He traveled the world
with the tour. He was well-read and erudite. But
he led the life of a black in Boston, where he
worked as a janitor after being trained as a teacher.
My mother's from South Boston. She claims she's

English, but we all think the bottom line's Irish.

My parents had enough to struggle with. One child was enough. They couldn't comfortably support more. I didn't notice anything different about my upbringing until I started growing up. I watched people watching my parents as we drove along in the car. In Boston at that time, it certainly wasn't unusual to come to a stop sign and have a couple in the car next to you staring at you. My parents were pretty aggressive, so they'd stare right back at them.

I have absolutely no regrets about being an only child. I liked the responsibility and independence of it. You get into trouble for everything, but you also get praised for everything. I had my own keys when I was six years old. I guess you could say I was sort of an early latch-key kid. My father worked nights, and my mother worked days, so someone would be home, but my father might be sleeping. My parents gave me a lot of independence quite early.

I really had to be imaginative because I didn't have other kids to play with. My parents forced me to read quite a bit. I was writing book reports on *Gulliver's Travels* when I was nine, not that I understood what it was about. My parents would send me to the Boston Public Library after school to occupy myself. If I got bored in the children's room, I'd just go roam the library.

Being an only child made me extremely calculating. I had to defend myself when trouble brewed. So I lied my way through ages nine to fourteen. I made up incredible stories all the time.

My parents would catch me at it, and I'd get into trouble, so I may have been doing it to get attention.

At the same time, I worried about how to really know people. I saw a lot of kids from larger families spending all their social energy on dealing with other members of the family. They'd take that out onto the street and spend their time battling with their friends. Since I didn't have anyone to play with at home, I had to be really affable. I wasn't looking for brothers and sisters, but I got pretty close to my friends pretty quickly. At one point, I really wanted to sleep over at other people's houses a lot. I wanted to hack around. That's what I feel I missed.

My father had been an athlete when he was young. And that was how we'd fill a lot of afternoons. I gravitated naturally to athletics. I loved to play sports, but I have some of the least competitive urgings. In a sense, as an only child, I never had anyone to compete against. I was just trying to be as good as I could for my parents, not for myself really. I realized later on that I'm not a team player. That may be why I gravitated toward pitching. I like solitary things. It didn't bother me at all to have pressure, because my parents were never satisfied with anything but the best.

My parents were pretty demanding. They expected a lot from me. Living next to a graduate dorm, I had taken so many psychological tests. Every time, the people giving the tests would tell my parents that I was very bright. When I was in the fifth grade in the Boston public school system and wasn't doing very well, they had me formally tested for the first time by a psychologist in Cambridge. They read lots of child psychology books, so they were on top of everything. After two days of tests, my parents realized the Boston schools didn't have much to offer, and they started to search out scholarships to other schools. It was a big time for prep schools to be courting inner-city blacks. The psychologist, who was pretty well-connected to private schools, said I was in the top 1 percent of ten-year-olds in the country. My parents were thrilled, and I went to the Belmont Hill School on scholarship.

I think it may be the curse of being an only child to always be trying to figure yourself out. I'm not sure that I care to be a member of a club that accepts me. I sort of like being an outcast. And I've probably been pushed toward it. I've been the first black in a lot of places. I went to one of these really ritzy summer camps in Wolfeboro, New Hampshire, and I was the first black. Yet, I definitely consider myself in my own class, with the acknowledgment that I'm considered a black by others. There's no way I could convince anyone in the larger social scale that I'm anything but black, just because of my physical appearance. At the same time, I'm not black and I'm not white. That, coupled with being an only child, makes me pretty arrogant in some ways.

My grades out of Belmont Hill were so-so, because I took advantage of the fact that they were interested in having a student-athlete. As an only child, the thing that I learned was to become perceptive. As a student-athlete, I perceived I could do anything.

After Belmont Hill, I went to Dartmouth. I went for a year, and it was the worst year of my life. Dartmouth was too much of a fraternity school. Dartmouth was the first place I ever tried to belong to a group. And the group I tried to belong to, just because I was pressed into it, was the Afro-Am Society. I've known maybe three blacks well in my life. I've never been around blacks. We never lived in Roxbury. So here I was, this sort of preppy kid. What happened at Dartmouth was that all the blacks wanted to make as if they came from the inner city, so they acted really funky and pretended their lives had really been rotten. Now these kids were ten times as wealthy as I was. Their parents were doctors, educated people. It blew me away. I didn't understand it at all.

I left Dartmouth after a year. I think my father stopped expecting things from me when I left. That was such a disappointment to him. They made a lot of sacrifices for me to go there. Dartmouth changed its scholarship allowance for me and really strained my parents' budget. They thought I really kicked them in the teeth by leaving Dartmouth. They gave me five hundred bucks and told me "good luck." I had worked in a clothing store in Boston, and for some reason, I just knew I could get a job in Brooks Brothers if I came down to New York. I got a job in forty minutes. I know how to make myself attractive.

That's what I mean by calculating. Then I came to *Time* magazine and got a job as a copyboy.

I didn't go back to school until five years later. Going back to college late was actually the first time I impressed myself. I don't have high self-esteem. I think well of myself, but it's built on a fairly shaky psyche. Being an only child, you're so full of potential that it becomes a curse. When I went back, I went to Pace University just to see how I liked school again. I did well, so I decided to go to Columbia. I had reached a point at twenty-five, when I really wanted an education. I was also old enough to be the outcast. It's easy to drift away from a group of teenagers when you're twenty-five. I could go to school and be mysterious to them. I could easily talk and chat with people at lunch, but still be a little distanced from them and be very happy. Even though I was at Columbia for three years, I don't know ten people from my class.

I hate traditionalism. My parents never married, so I lived with one name for twelve years and then changed names between seventh and eighth grades. I was Jimmy Williams all the way through seventh grade. I have no interest in history. I think that's partially the result of being an only child and the son of an only child. I don't have any aunts or uncles on my father's side of the family. I think my father's mother was fourteen when she had him. I don't think my father has a history that he particularly wants to tell. My mother was alienated from her brothers and sisters, except for one. So I really don't have aunts and uncles on that side.

But my son Matt will learn history because of his mother's family, the Fulhams. My wife, Mary, is from a family of five kids. Larger families care about the family tree. We were home for Christmas in Boston last year, and Mary got all this family information from my mother in the course of ten minutes. My mother pulled out her scrapbook of when she was a girl. I like being married, and I love having a son. But I feel sort of uncomfortable belonging to the Fulham family. To me, it's a little too large and they're a little too informed about each other. They really care too much.

Without negating my parents, I've always had a sense of coming this far alone. I love them, but I'm terrible about calling home. If Mary didn't call them or they didn't call me, I'd let a month go by easily. Now with the grandson, they're calling constantly. I fantasize now and then about what life would be like without my parents. Aside from the immediate feeling of loss, my first instinct is that I'd finally be able to be myself.

The whole thing about my life to this point is that everything has been at diametric poles: my parents, my upbringing. I went to summer camp, private schools, Dartmouth, yet I'm from a middle- to lower-middle-class family. Everything has been just such a contradiction.

I think I really work too hard to achieve this sense of self-sufficiency. I'm not saying I'm not a good team player because I don't know how to play on teams. But even when I am playing on a team, I'll make myself different in some way from my teammates so that they know it, even if the coach doesn't. I find it easy to be different. I strive for it. I think that being an only child, that sense of oneness, makes you want to be unique in other situations.

seven

SUCCESS AND THE SINGLE CHILD

*T*he best thing I could do was to do well. In everything. From an early age, I was paid off for good grades. An "A" was worth a dollar from three sources: aunt and uncle, father, and grandparents. To me, praise was worth almost as much. I wanted to be perfect. I couldn't stand it if I felt I was doing something wrong—or trying to do something I couldn't accomplish.

At the age of ten or so, I decided I wanted to learn how to play the piano, even though my family didn't own one. There was a club in the neighborhood, the Brotherhood Club, that had a piano. I would go there and practice by myself. Even after my father gave me a piano for Christmas and I could practice in the comfort of my home, I used all those years of practicing in an empty building to justify not wanting to play in front of anyone. The truth was that I couldn't stand to let anyone hear all the mistakes I made. Every time I was forced to play the piano in front of

168

anyone at all my hands would start to shake, my pulse would quicken, and I would stumble all over the keyboard.

Scholastically, I knew that, except in math, there really was no such thing as perfection, only relative excellence. But I learned to set goals early. I coveted a Sawyer Medal, a small pin and medallion imprinted with the face of the founder of Gloucester's library. Each year Sawyer Medals were awarded to the top ten students in the eighth grade; two were awarded to students each year in high school. I steadfastly kept my average up, awaiting my day of triumph. Sure enough, on the day of the junior high graduation, I walked up on stage to accept my Sawyer Medal. It probably had a different significance for me than for some of the other winners. My mother had not won her Sawyer Medal until she had been a freshman in high school. I had won mine a year earlier. I had finally outdone my mother, a competition I had engaged in, at least in my mind, for some time.

Credentials began to be important to me. I started collecting them after I won my Sawyer Medal. In high school, I became editor of the newspaper and the literary magazine. I made it a practice to do only those things I thought I could do well. I dropped fourth-year French because it might ruin my academic average. I didn't take marine biology because I had had a hard time in chemistry. I didn't even consider taking physics. I wanted to score a grand slam when I applied to colleges. But my real love was the extracurriculars. I missed only one day of high school, not because I wanted a perfect attendance record or I enjoyed all my classes, but because if I didn't go to school, I couldn't go in and work on the newspaper.

At Mount Holyoke, I continued to do what I thought I could do well. In my freshman English seminar, the teacher, a young, earthy man everyone admired, assigned our first paper. The next week, he told the class that we were all close to illiterate "with the possible exception of one student." I was that student. I had talent, I thought. I must major in English, I decided, although political science had been my plan. I wrote a review for the student newspaper, Choragos, and the editor took me aside and told me it was the best in any of the Five-College newspapers.

Like the chosen one, I dedicated myself to writing and journalism. I thrived on praise.

When I was graduating from Mount Holyoke, my classmates selected me to give the baccalaureate address. The subject was excellence. Two faculty members were also speaking. Tom Reese, who was retiring, was one of the great favorites at Holyoke. He taught a beginning psych course that people would attend even if they weren't enrolled. His final class always had to be moved into a larger lecture hall so that hordes of students could hear him sum up what mattered in psychology and life. He preceded me, alas, to the podium, regal in his ermine-edged gown from Cambridge. His speech, not unexpectedly, was much better than mine. The audience's applause was thunderous. My stomach started turning. I began to sweat. I hoped I'd be struck by a bolt of lightning. There was no way to win, to be the best, so I just tried to get through it as best I could. After I had finished to polite applause and the ceremony was over, my boyfriend, to whom I had assigned the role of critic, told me that I had mispronounced two words. Later that day, after I graduated magna cum laude, an accomplishment that strained me more than anyone could ever know, my aunt told me nonchalantly: "Oh, I wasn't surprised. I expected you to graduate with honors." I felt little urge to celebrate.

So I sailed off to New York to start a career, always trying my hardest. I felt there was safety in excellence. I thought if I did good work, I would always have a job. If I had a job, I could take care of myself. A lot of the drive came down to fear and the knowledge that ultimately no one could provide for me except myself. And in the back of my mind I wanted to accomplish things because if I died at thirty-eight, like my mother did, I wanted to have a full life to my credit.

A couple of years ago, I was invited back to Mount Holyoke to receive an award that is given to four alumnae each year for distinguishing themselves in their careers. The other recipients that year were a banker, a writer of science fiction, and an opera singer. It turned out that three out of four of us were only children. We talked about being only children and what success means to us—and what it costs. As I left the campus, it struck me that the ultimate achievement is knowing when enough is enough.

One of the few positive stereotypes connected to the only child is that of the high achiever. The Apollo astronauts are largely responsible. In the late 1960s, someone noted that twenty-one out of the twenty-three Apollo astronauts were either firstborn or only children. These men were national heroes, lionized by the press, admired by the American public. They were the best and the brightest. They had the "right stuff." They were everything only children were purported not to be. *Time* magazine chose the Apollo 8 astronauts, William Anders, Frank Borman, and James Lovell, for its Man of the Year cover in 1968. All three were only children.

"I think if I hadn't been an only child, I wouldn't be where I am today," says William Anders, who is now senior executive vice-president of the Textron Corporation in Rhode Island. "Being an only child was part of the background that led to the Naval Academy. If I had had an older brother, I might have had less response to my dad's unstated but clearly visible wish that I follow in his footsteps as a naval officer and Naval Academy graduate. Ironically, I went into the air force. But at least I was in the military. Something caused me to lean toward aviation. Perhaps I was a little less afraid than, say, two little brothers might be, of walking into a cave alone. I had to go out and explore on my own. Something led me to become an engineer as well, maybe because I played by myself and had to invent my own bridges instead of playing tic-tac-toe with siblings. So probably all those things fit together. How do I know which one had the impact?"

Anders says that fellow astronauts and pilots were quite aware of all the birth-order studies in the sixties. "It was quite the thing when we were down in the space program," recalls Anders. "As I look at my fighter-pilot colleagues, there are two traits you find a lot. One is the firstborn son, the other is the runt. If you've got a firstborn runt, you've got one of the best fighter pilots going—although no fighter pilot would ever admit he was a runt."

Did the three Apollo 8 astronauts talk about being only children as they circled the earth? "That community shied away from philosophical talk," says Anders. "It was not the right stuff to do that. Macho runts don't even suggest there's anything going on besides what supreme beings they are. You didn't get much introspective talk. It was a sign of weakness. Since it was such a topic in the press in those days, it was hard to figure out what was actually an original idea or awareness versus what somebody put in your mind."

James Lovell, a fellow astronaut who is now executive vice-president at the Centel Corporation in Chicago, says that he believes that the number of only children in the space program had a lot to do with the fact that most of the men were born during the Depression, when only children were common. "We talked about being only children," he recalls. "But we didn't see any similarities. If you talk to all three of us, you'll see three completely different personalities and ways of operation—although I think that all three of us were fairly successful in second careers." Indeed, in addition to Anders's and Lovell's success in business, Frank Borman, the third Apollo 8 astronaut, went on to become president of Eastern Airlines. Concludes Lovell: "If you want to look for something in common, there was a drive to be successful, not just in the space program but after we left. Some astronauts are still trying to find their way in life. But we just took off and found our own way."

* * *

More and more studies provide anecdotal evidence that only children and firstborns finish first. Walter and Eleonore Toman of Brandeis University surveyed "distinguished persons" who were on the covers of *Time* magazine from 1957 to 1968. Among 215 men selected, 59 had been oldest sons and 58 had been onlies. Of the 36 women who had been on the covers, 14 had been the oldest and seven were onlies. The researchers concluded that oldest siblings and only children appeared more frequently on the *Time* covers than by chance, and that middle siblings were clearly underrepresented. "We suspect," wrote the Tomans, "that both oldest siblings and single children tend to have been more intimately identified with their parents than middle or younger siblings. This great training in identification with parents and parental goals may help them in their careers. They can identify better than middle and youngest siblings with those in authority, with institutions, and with internalized goals which authorities and institutions like."

List makers note that such diverse world leaders as Alexander the Great, Josef Stalin, Queen Victoria, Indira Gandhi, and Franklin D. Roosevelt were only children. Esquire magazine, which celebrates American leaders under forty, observed in 1985 that half of the people selected were either firstborn or only children. Korn/Ferry International, a leading executive search firm, and the UCLA Graduate School of Management surveyed senior executives at America's largest corporations. Of these executives, 14 percent were only children. An even more surprising fact: America's two top corporate raiders, T. Boone Pickens and Carl Icahn, are both only children.

It would seem that only children begin their assault on success early, both by nature and nurture. Project TALENT, the major study that tracked high school students, found that only children showed a marked inclination to pursue sciences, music, math, and writing, while children with a sibling indicated more of an interest in sports, outdoor work, skilled trades, labor, mechanical work, and office work.

Why do only children gravitate toward the white-collar, cerebral occupations, while young people with siblings are more interested in manual and outdoor pursuits? Project TALENT found a pattern that combined "higher academic skills, particularly verbal skills, with a greater need to achieve academically." The researchers conclude: "First, only children performed at a higher intellectual level than non-only children. It could be expected, then, that they would tend to choose occupations calling for thought as opposed to manual labor. Second, it has long been postulated that only children receive an exaggerated amount of parental attention and encouragement to achieve. Although this parental drive may have negative effects, it may also instill in only children a desire to obtain the maximum possible education and a tendency to gravitate toward the more socially prestigious occupations." The study also found that girls who were only children had significantly higher college expectations than girls who were not. When Project TALENT did its ten-year follow-up, these expectations had been achieved: Female onlies had gone farther in college than women with a sibling.

The parents of only children seem to be very supportive when it comes to providing opportunity and education. UCLA Professor Judith Blake found that an only child is likely to get three more years of education than a child with several siblings. That education can help speed the only child toward success.

Toni Falbo, an educational psychologist who has devoted her career to the study of only children, believes that researchers have never done the proper critical analysis to determine whether there are, in fact, a disproportionate number of prominent people who are only children. "People of higher socioeconomic status tend to have fewer children, so they're more likely to have only one child," says Falbo. "On top of that, people who come from higher socioeconomic status are more likely to achieve. Why do people have just one child? You might have parents who are very achievement-oriented themselves and they're not particularly interested in having a lot of kids because they're busy doing X, Y, and Z. If so, then what they teach their only child is that what's important in life is to achieve. So there's an issue of value-transmission." Falbo believes that it is a combination of all the social factors, rather than simply being an only child, that pushes a person toward achieving. "The achievement of an only child increases over time because the income of the parents increases, and the only child has more resources to draw on for special tutoring, college, and money to invest in first businesses," concludes Falbo.

In *The Great American Success Story,* a survey of successful people chosen from the pages of Marquis's *Who's Who in America,* George Gallup, Jr. and Alec M. Gallup investigated traits that lead to success. They found that supportive parents are key. So is self-reliance, the desire to excel, and the ability to set goals. The Gallups also found that successful people tend to be avid readers. Sounds familiar.

At its best, parental support can give an only child the tools and self-confidence to reach his potential. Dr. Walter Bortz, an expert on geriatrics who practices in Palo Alto, California, was the son of a prominent physician in Philadelphia. Bortz says he went into medicine because he never thought of anything else. "I revered my dad," says Bortz.

"He was a god in my eyes." Bortz found academics easy. "I was the alpha male in all my classes," he says. "I was the best student. I was very aggressive. My parents didn't push me. It was totally inner drive. My folks' technique was praise, saying how well you're doing, that you're terrific. So it was not ever a threat or anything."

Bortz thinks that it is no accident that he specializes in geriatrics, since his parents were relatively old when he was born. In fact, he has a strong sense of good fortune and predestination. "I knew I'd be a successful doctor," he says. "I knew I would marry a pretty girl, I knew I'd have some kids. I knew the things that would be a part of my life. I think I could have shut my eyes when I was ten and pretty much sat down and written my biography."

Bortz was fortunate that the life he chose was similar to the one that his parents might have picked for him. But for other only children, parental expectations can be overbearing. As one only child points out: "If you're going to Exeter, you're going there to succeed. If you're going to Princeton, it's because great things are expected of you." Some parents allow little room for failure. Flip Spiceland, the meteorologist with CNN, says, "I had that typical situation where if I got a 98, Dad said what's wrong with a 100? And they still do. I've never been a particularly ambitious person, and I've always been satisfied with what I had. But it's never enough. In anything I did, it didn't matter what it was, they were pushing me constantly."

Indeed, some only children often become achievers because they are expected to be all things to two people. The expectations can start early. "I was pressed to be better than anyone else," says one only child. "When I was five or six, I had lessons at the Curtis School of Elocution on Commonwealth Avenue in Boston. They had a recital of *Snow White and the Seven Dwarfs,* and I was one of the dwarfs. All the other dwarfs got the flu, so I played all seven dwarfs and was particularly annoyed because they didn't ask me to play Snow White, too. I was ready to take on any role."

Many parents invest too much of their egos into their only child, who is expected to be the family ambassador to the world, and, like any diplomat, to have impeccable deportment and manners. Although he liked being an only child, Bill Brennan, the television and theatrical producer, recalls that perfection was an elusive goal. "I was supposed to be perfect, the best," he says. "I couldn't act up like other kids could because, after all, my dad was an attorney in the town. That developed a lot of tension for me. If another kid fouled up, that was one thing, but Billy Brennan couldn't. At one point, for instance, I became ineligible to play in one football game because I got a D in geometry. My father said, 'How can I expect people to come do law business with me when my son isn't eligible to play?' That was a terrible week. And the teacher was in worse shape. She told me: 'If I ever knew it was going to cause this, I never would have done it. I was just trying to shape you up.' There was no area for me to goof, to foul up."

Some parents have high expectations whether they have one child or three, but the screws seem to turn a little tighter on one child. Expectations can be pretty far-reaching, extending well beyond academics. Lawyer Ruth Ainslie says, "I felt enormous pressure. Because I was an only child, I had to be everything. I had to be a good student. I had to be professionally successful. And I had to get married. I had to have children. It's as if parents want one of everything for their only child, when the wealth might be better spread among many. In my husband's family, everyone seems to have a different role. This one does this, that one does that.

As long as there's a great student, this one doesn't have to be. If one is creative, the other can be athletic. Out of four children, there was someone to fulfill every need. I felt enormous pressure to be good in everything."

Bill Brennan concurs: "I played football, basketball, baseball, track. I was in the school plays. Finally, I decided I just wasn't going to do it anymore. When I took myself out of all that, Mother said, 'But honey, you did so well!' Friends love the story about Lucille Ball. She was doing a musical in New York called *Wildcat.* A friend of mine, an actor, was talking about the show, describing a part. Kiddingly, I said, 'That's not your part, I'm the guy who should be playing that part.' He said, 'You're right.' So he called Lucy, whom I knew. Lucy called me one day and said: 'Get your ass over here. I want to talk to you.' So I went over to her house and she gave me the script. Of course, I couldn't take the role. I wasn't an actor. But the key thing is, my mother said afterward, 'Oh, honey, if you had only kept up with your singing!' "

It seems as if some parents of only children are never satisfied. Achievement can become a life-long treadmill. Even if the child has achieved his or her own expectations, parents may still want more. One successful journalist wrote a book that she did not particularly want to write because her aging parents kept complaining that they wanted her to dedicate a book to them before they died.

William Anders, the Apollo astronaut, chortles about his parents' continuing interest. "Even though I'm in my fifties, my parents focus a lot of attention and expect a lot out of their boy," he says. "I'm totally satisfied. I figure I could quit right now, and I'm ahead of the game. I guess they think so, too. But they still take pride in Bill getting a new job or something. They always asked me why don't I run for this or for that, and I always told them it was a lousy job."

*   *   *

Many only children succeed because of a subtle combination of expectations and sense of self. A good parental example can be very positive. "Coming from a professional family, I never thought of becoming anything but a professional," says Katherine Feinstein, an assistant district attorney in San Francisco. "I had some great educational advantages. A lot of good things I accomplished have been because I was pushed to accomplish them, and I was expected to accomplish them. The thing is, I wasn't pushed very hard. I was one of those kids who they never had to tell to study. They never had to tell me I couldn't watch television, because I didn't think of watching television. I was very motivated academically all on my own."

Only children, growing up with the idea that they must rely on themselves, may take extra steps to ensure their place in the world. The desire to excel becomes more of a sense of self-preservation. Joseph Mawson, a forestry professor at the University of Massachusetts, was the first in his family to go to college. "The pressure didn't come from them," he says. "It came from me. I figured I'd better do something because I'm the only child. I'm the only one. I've got to go to college. I've got to be successful. My dad expects me to be. My dad never said so. It was the way he ran his own life. To him, hard work was very important. Loyalty was very important. My mother always said, 'Think for yourself.' " What Mawson thought was: "They pay you more for using your brains than for using your brawn." So he got degrees from Duke, Berkeley, and the University of Maine. "They don't pay you for walking through the woods on hikes," he laughs. "They pay you for writing papers and doing research."

Sometimes only children drive themselves to accomplish things because they feel that something is lacking in their

lives. They try to distinguish themselves because they have
a complex need to overcompensate. Gail Roper, who swam
for the U.S. in the 1952 Olympics, suffered for years because
her father left home when she was six months old and her
mother had little interest in her abilities. "I guess I always
had a chip on my shoulder," says Roper. "I grew up thinking
I was less than all the other children."

Roper began swimming at the age of two and did not get
much encouragement until high school. She did not start
winning, however, until she was out on her own. "After I
graduated, I decided I would compete again. I was allowed
to use the pool, but I swam by myself. I really didn't know
what training was. My father came home for the big meet.
In my mind, I felt if I won that my father would stay. It
meant everything to me. My mother and father were there,
and so were my grandparents. But I came in fourth. I was so
crushed, I went into the locker room and cried and cried. The
janitor finally took me home. My father was gone, and my
mother didn't speak to me. I felt like such a failure. I decided
I was going to do something about it."

So Roper started reading everything she could about
swimming and the training of top swimmers. "Nowhere
along the line did I think I'd make the Olympics or be a
national champion," she says. "No one really cared. No one
ever said you can do it. It wasn't so much that I had confidence in my abilities as, well, I did a 1:23 and this other girl
did a 1:22. I bet I can do a 1:22. There were all these little
incentives to go a little bit faster, a little bit faster." Roper
was twenty-three when she was in the Olympics. Although
she did not win a medal, she later set a world record for the
breaststroke in 1953.

Roper got married at twenty-seven and began having her
seven children. "My husband thought I should be a house-

wife," she says. "So I decided to become the best housewife possible. I learned how to decorate the house, how to cook. I was such a good wife. I sewed my daughter's clothes, sewed curtains, decorated. I wanted everyone to know what a good mother, wife, cook, and interior decorator I was. I wasn't happy. It wasn't enough. I felt I should be doing more. I believed that the better you got, the happier you'd be. It was like being on a treadmill. Every Christmas the children had to get more presents than the year before. The turkey had to be bigger."

In 1970, at the age of forty-one, Roper dove into swimming again, partly to reclaim her life. Since then, she has set more than fifty records in her age group. At the age of fifty-six, she recorded her fastest time ever for the butterfly. "I've always wanted to achieve something great," says Roper. "When I was winning all those national championships, nobody knew. I set a world record in every single event. I did it, and nobody knew, but I knew."

For many only children, the desire to excel is as natural as getting up in the morning. Roger Staubach, the legendary quarterback for the Dallas Cowboys, says that his drive was completely internal. "I had a drive inside of me that was different," he says. "I guess perseverance is the key element in anyone's life, the ability to just never quit. When things are going in the wrong direction, people have a tendency to pull back. I've always had a tendency to push forward, push harder."

As Staubach got older, he began planning for what he would do after his football career was over. "There are a lot of good qualities you can transfer from the athletic field to the business world," he maintains. "But you must understand that just having those qualities is not enough. You have to lay the groundwork and the foundation like you do as an athlete. The vision of looking down the road is very difficult when you're paid a lot of money. As an athlete, you're pampered and your life's needs are pretty well taken care of. You're living from one season to the next. Obviously, it's going to end. I was very prepared for the end. I got started in the real estate business, recognizing that if I wanted another profession someday, I'd have to get some sort of foundation for it. So I spent eleven years of giving my entire off-season to real estate. The Staubach Company has had a great deal of success. We've done some developing, and it's a big headache right now. I think adversity reveals genius and prosperity conceals it. You find out how smart you are when times are the toughest."

For Staubach high expectations have never been a burden. "I've got some areas of my life that maybe are attributable to being an only child that I'm awfully glad I have," he says. "Qualities like drive, competitiveness, and the desire to please my parents. When I grew up playing football, baseball, and basketball, I had the desire to be the best that I could be at what I was doing. If I could take away those things and trade them for two or three brothers or sisters, I wouldn't. I'm pleased with my life."

For many only children, a spirit of independence helps them to keep a perspective on success. Katherine Feinstein, whose mother became mayor of San Francisco, will admit that her parents thought "that I would be happy if I did more with my life than I might have done if left to my own devices." Now married and challenged by her job as an assistant district attorney, she is indeed happy. "I like to work in my garden, and I like to go out to dinner with my friends," she says. "I don't ever want to be a Supreme Court justice. I don't ever want to be in Mensa. I don't ever want to have the biggest house or the best wardrobe. I don't want to starve. My mother goes nuts. She says, 'I want you to come here and meet so and so.' And I will say, 'What am I going to say to so and so?' There are certain people you were only meant to read about. I get pleasure out of my cat, my garden. My little life makes me very happy. In a way, my mother would probably react to that as a lack of ambition. My mother has plans for me to run for various offices, how it's all going to be organized. But I am not very ambitious. If the people I know feel their lives are a little better because of the part I played, I'm happy. That's all I really want."

A TALE

Clint, * *mid-forties, photographer, New York City:*

I definitely had the feeling that I was the different kid on the block. I grew up in a very ethnic neighborhood, predominantly Irish and Italian. The families ranged from three kids, to one around the corner with nine. What made my situation even more different was that my father died when I was eighteen months old. So it was just me and my mother. She never chose to remarry. She was working all the time, so I was really isolated.

I definitely had a sense of being alone. I guess it motivated me in a lot of different ways to become tough, to fight to survive, to fight to get ahead, to be the leader of the gang, to be the best on the baseball team, to be the best on the football team. There was always a motivation to excel.

*A pseudonym

Perhaps it was because I felt I had less than others. Perhaps it was because of the lack of support and relatives that I wanted my friends to look up to me.

It wasn't just in good ways. For instance, there was a place up by Baker Field at the tip of Manhattan where we'd go swimming in the Harlem River. We used to jump off the cut down there. There was always a point at which you'd try to go a little higher and a little higher. I always tried to go the highest, just to have people look up to me. It was rather dangerous sometimes. One day, someone jumped off and never came up. They found him stuck in a garbage can at the bottom of the river. But that never deterred me from going higher. That started very young, back in grade school. It really did help, looking back, to formulate my motivations later.

By the time I was a teenager, the Bronx had become a tough, tough area. The gangs that everyone feared and heard about from that period of time were all concentrated in my area. I lived in the West Bronx, near Fordham Road. At that time, you had several choices of how you were going to direct the course of your life. Most of it was directed toward crime, petty crime sometimes. People were shooting heroin. A lot of people were alcoholics by the time they were seventeen. On weekends we used to drink anywhere from six to twelve quarts of beer per body. Everybody started smoking regular cigarettes when they were ten and were smoking grass by the time they were fourteen. Some were sent to prison for grand larceny. Stealing cars was the big thing. Breaking into stores was another thing. Once you got inside reform school or prison, there wasn't much chance for rehabilitation. I saw it happen all the time.

I was engaged at the age of eighteen to a girl who was sixteen years old. Her father was a lieutenant of the Mafia. When you grew up in that kind of atmosphere, one of your dreams was to become a member of the mob. It was really part of life there. Anyone's family who was in the Mafia lived better than anyone else. They had all the flashy cars, all the flashy jewelry, all the flashy women, and lived an exciting life, most of which you read about in the newspapers or saw on television in *The Untouchables.* They had the best of everything.

Going out with this girl, I became more and more involved with her family. When we got engaged, her father began taking me on some of his rounds. We'd do collections on loan-shark deals. He would make all these collections from people who beg on the streets, blind people. It was a scam because none of these people were blind. So we'd go around to newsstand dealers, and he would get a percentage because they were in his district. He had a lot of after-hours clubs, gay clubs, and he had big plans for me. He put me into a construction crew he was involved with. Between working on the construction crew daytimes and collecting at night with him, I was eighteen years old and making seven hundred to eight hundred dollars a week. It was a lot of money back then. I had a great, big, flashy black-and-yellow convertible. I was on the way. You could go into hard crime and probably get arrested, or you could deal drugs—or you could get into the Mob.

The thing that may have put me off on that whole life was the whole thing about worrying when you'd be caught. We were sitting in a car one Sunday afternoon, myself and this Mafia guy's daughter and her two sisters. A rival gang threatened us and turned over the car we were in. There were four of us and ten of them. A couple of nights later, I was called to this meeting. I was asked to go with a group of people and point out who the people were. I was pretty angry, too, that they had threatened us. We went up to this pool-room in eight cars. I got out of the car and looked into the poolroom, came back to the car, and said that the ten were all in there. The windows in four of the cars behind me went down, and it was like an atomic bomb went off. They blew the whole place up. It was slaughter. One person died, one person lost a leg. It was pretty frightening. I came to the reality: Maybe there's something else out there. That was the turning point for me. As often as I had dreamed of being Edward G. Robinson or George Raft or being a Mafioso, that day really shook me up.

I left home, which I did frequently. I used to disappear just to get away. I went away for a week, to the beach, and thought about my life and what I wanted to do and why I had chosen at this age this particular thing. And I just decided: I don't want to be like everyone else. I've never been like everybody else, and I'm not going to start now. As much money as I had been making, as much as I could make, it wasn't important. I just saw myself going to jail or being killed in gang wars. So I broke off the engagement and had to leave New York for a while. I came back and got involved with another Italian girl, who I married six months later. We had a child eight months later.

I had dropped out of high school in my junior year and then went back and finished. Then I went to night school at Columbia while working three jobs to support my wife and child. I found a job in a publishing company, and I sold *Life* magazine on the phone at night. I worked in the post office on the weekends. I'd go to Columbia three times a week. And it was difficult to make that transition, especially coming from a very free and easy life. I had a family and suddenly no money at all.

For the first couple of years, I wondered what made me do that, give that all up, to lead a straight life. I guess it really went back to being an only child. I always had this incredible sense of independence growing up. I always did what I wanted to do, not what others wanted me to do, whether it was my mother, or the nuns or priests at Catholic school. My friends couldn't understand. They'd say: "You had it made, Tony will kill you now." They didn't understand it. Nobody had it better than me in terms of status and money. But I guess it was my sense of independence that said to me: This isn't what you should be doing; to hell with everybody else; to hell with Tony. I had to do what my instincts told me. I don't think I would have had those instincts if I hadn't grown up by myself with nobody to turn to. There were no brothers and sisters, no father. So I had to listen to myself a lot of the time. And that's what made me do it.

That sense of being independent and responsible for myself had a lot to do with my maturing early as a photojournalist. I look at other photographers who came out of the same generation and had the same opportunities or even more and didn't take advantage of them. Or maybe they didn't know how to take advantage of them. I don't ever regret being an only child. It gave me a sense of ambition and a need to succeed. I took all sorts of chances on the way up in the hope of reaching new plateaus.

eight

MERGING:

MARRIAGE

AND

CHILDREN

I used to think that the best way to travel through life was alone, unencumbered and uncompromised. I valued close friendships, but I saw marriage as a threat. I spent so many years trying to be self-sufficient that I was afraid of being forever diminished by making the wrong choice of a husband. During my twenties, I had long relationships and painful partings. As I moved closer to thirty, though, I began to want to share my life.

Deep down, I was looking for a man who came from the kind of family I lacked. I was curious about sibling relationships. Whenever I was dating a man, I assessed his family. I would compare a boyfriend's mother with what I thought my own mother might have become. I wondered whether his sister could become the sister I never had. And whenever a relationship with a man ended, my more lasting regret always seemed to be over losing his family.

More than anything else, though, I wanted to find someone who longed for a partnership that could combine intimacy and individuality. I found this person in a man I had known for a number of years but had never dated. It was his golden retriever personality, sweet and gentle, that made him so endearing. Besides, we had a lot in common. We were both journalists. We both understood the precariousness of life because we each had lost a parent when we were young. Although our temperaments were opposite, our values about work and life were similar. He was a feminist, in part because he had grown up with a very strong and independent mother. His sister was warm and welcoming. She later told me that she, too, had been looking for a sister.

Paul and I seemed to see eye to eye on the important things—at least until the night when we casually started talking about children. I told him that if I had any, I wanted only one. He told me that he would rather have none than one because he thought that only children were spoiled. I didn't speak to him for several hours, furious that someone who knew me so well could say something so thoughtless. He apologized the next day and promised to be more open-minded.

When we announced that we were going to get married, my friends were ecstatic. They had been extolling the comforts of marriage to me for a couple of years. My family was relieved that finally, at the age of thirty-one, I was making the commitment. They had never put any real pressure on me to get married and have children. I think they were secretly pleased that I was so happy with my life and work in New York. But as my stepmother put it: "Life's a lot more fun if you have someone to share it with."

At the time we got married, Paul was living in Detroit, and I was living in New York. I thought this was a pretty good arrangement. We could both work hard during the week and concentrate on each other on the weekends. We had a lovely honeymoon in Italy. Arriving back at Kennedy Airport afterward, we took a cab to my apartment. (It was still, after all, my apartment. He had his in Detroit.) We unpacked the bags and divided up our purchases and clothes. Then he took a cab back to La

Guardia and flew off to Detroit. It was sad for a few moments, maybe even a day or so. But it gave us some time to get used to the idea of being married before we had to cope, after many years of living alone, with the tougher challenge of living together.

A few months later, I won a fellowship at the University of Michigan and took a leave of absence from Time *magazine. We began living together in earnest, but the adjustment was not as difficult as I had expected. He gave me first dibs on closets, and since I had the most clothes, I got the biggest one. Dinners were a bit more difficult. I was an earlier eater, so I would snack at seven, then eat dinner with him at nine. I put on some weight, which made me unhappy. Soon, I realized that he did not expect us to do things, like eating, in tandem. I went back to setting my own agenda and including him when I could. I found it great to have a built-in companion.*

When the fellowship ended, we went back to our commuting. I was much more miserable this time. There would be a crisis during the week, and my comfort would have to come via Ma Bell. I came to loathe the battle to get to Newark Airport during rush hour on Fridays and the seven-thirty Northwest flight to Detroit, which served nothing but peanuts during the dinner hour. But I didn't want to live in Detroit, and he didn't want to live in New York. So we settled on San Francisco.

Now that we share a house together, I notice that we both have our little areas of privacy. You obviously don't have to be an only child to appreciate your own space. He spends hours in the basement puttering around. I have my office that he enters only in order to get to the coat closet. It's an equitable deal. I asked him recently if he still thinks that only children are spoiled. He said no, that I'm very easy to get along with. Nice guy.

As the myth goes, only children are not ideal marriage material. After all, they are not trained from infancy to share rooms and possessions. And they tend to value privacy and independence, two potential enemies of intimacy. Despite their streaks of independence, though, only children appear to be as successful at marriage and parenthood as anybody else. Because they do not take relationships for granted, only children often try harder. If anything, they may feel a greater need to marry in order to extend their family. In his book *Raising the Only Child,* Dr. Murray Kappelman notes: "The only child can make a superb marriage partner . . . The ability to have the other person so close after long years of aloneness often makes the only child an eager, caring, almost overly solicitous mate."

In their study of only children, Sharryl Hawke and David Knox asked single children whether their upbringing affected their marital relationships. The majority said no. But the 41 percent who answered yes, cited both positive and negative effects. Some only children thought they valued their spouse and his or her family more. On the other hand, some onlies cited problems involving needs for quiet time, privacy, and independence.

Only children seem to grow up expecting to get married, like most everyone else. Project TALENT questioned high school students about their hopes and found that non-onlies expected to marry sooner and to have more children than onlies. The eleven-year follow-up indicated that the non-onlies had done exactly that. However, Project TALENT also found that these people with a sibling were more likely than only children to be divorced at the age of twenty-nine. Although only children indicated that they planned to marry later and have smaller families, they actually married sooner than they expected—and they did follow through on the smaller families.

Only children marry for the same reasons other people do: love and money, chance and chemistry. "I always sort of wanted to be married one day," says Marni Weil, an only child who took the plunge after thirty. "There was no rush. And I would not have gotten married just to get married. I love being alone, and I miss being alone a lot. But I thought it would be nice one day to have someone to share my life with."

Some only children may also have a hidden agenda: acquiring a bigger and better family. It may be that only children look at the family "package" they are getting through marriage more than other people, who perhaps take brothers, sisters, nieces, and nephews more for granted. "If I married another only child, my children wouldn't have cousins," says Ruth Ainslie. "It's something I thought about maybe at age ten. That it would be very lonely, and it would not be fair."

"My husband is one of seven kids, so I was very aware that I was marrying a family," says Ann Fisher of San Francisco. "Steven and I were immediately attracted to each other. We share similarities in being the oldest and being take-charge types of people. When I married my husband, I had a fantasy of what that sort of family life would be like. And their family conforms to my ideal. It's fun to see some of the vibes that go between them."

Yet in acquiring the new family, an only child may have trouble loosening the ties to the old. Particularly if an only child is the hypotenuse to a family triangle, it may be very difficult to "forsake all others." Dr. Walter Bortz, who practices in California, had found it necessary to move from his birthplace, Philadelphia. "Ruth Anne was just twenty-two when we were married, and I was twenty-three," says Bortz. "When we got married, I was still my parents' child. I didn't forsake them. My mother's not an easy person. I identify with her well, but she's very demanding. With Ruth Anne she was scathing. But I was caught in the middle. I was practicing at the same hospital in Philadelphia that my father had built and was a very prestigious member of. When we left Philadelphia fifteen years ago, part of it was to escape this power of my mother."

Both men and women can experience difficulties as they distance themselves from devoted parents. "I think my parents hung on real tight," recalls one woman now in her late thirties. "And I think it was a two-way street. It was hard to break. My husband got real mad at me when we first got married because we would be going to visit my parents and I would say, 'We're going home this weekend.' He'd say, 'Dammit, that's not home. Your home is with me.' It took a while to get over that. There were a lot of bonds."

One woman, a teacher in New York state, says that her parents finally accepted what is now a fourteen-year relationship with another woman. "In the beginning it was horrible," she recalls. "The irony is it wouldn't really have mattered who the person was, male or female, because we were such a trio. There was such a feeling of the three musketeers that I think anyone who got in the way of the three of us would have been resented to a certain extent. Since this relationship precluded them from having grandchildren, it was very hard to deal with."

There are other problems that only children encounter as they marry. While only children tend to do very well in one-on-one relationships, it may require a special effort to share another person's feelings and concerns. Like everyone who gets married, only children have to make adjustments. It may be hard, for instance, for an independent only child to share a bedroom and bureau. Or it may be difficult to get the knack of moving in tandem with another person.

While many only children look forward to acquiring more family, sometimes large numbers of new relatives can be overwhelming. Lynne Humkey of Wilmore, Kentucky, finds that gatherings with her husband's family are too hectic. "My husband's one of seven boys," she says. "He's a twin, and he and his brother are extremely close. At holidays when everyone is together, I find I just want to get away. Everybody's talking, but nobody's listening. I just want to retreat somewhere and take a walk."

Katherine Feinstein, who has been married several years, admits to an intense sense of privacy. "I have a real thing about somebody coming to my house," she says. "If somebody gets invited to my house, it's because I really trust them. It is not because I have a great TV and stereo that I think someone is going to steal. It's because my house is my little world. If my husband called to say he was bringing someone home for dinner, I would not be there when he got there and I wouldn't come back. He might as well tell me he's found an eighteen-year-old blonde, and he's moving to Hawaii."

While most only children get married, deciding to have a child may be a harder issue. As I talked to only children, I realized that they were passionately divided on the subject of children. Some felt that they simply had to have at least one child because of the desire for a blood relative. Others felt they lacked the background or motivation to become a parent.

Only children who feel they missed out on something seem to put a high priority on having children, usually in the plural. "I think I lost out on a lot in my childhood," says Laura Stein-Stapleford. "Shortly after I delivered my first child, I had two things in mind. Number one, I'm not going to have an only child. Two, I want my child to have everything I didn't have as a child—somebody else to goof off with while we're waiting for a table in a restaurant, somebody to play Candyland with, somebody who will be a companion." While her two children seem to have those things, Stein-Stapleford admits that there are trade-offs. "Sometimes I feel guilty because I think I am not giving either child the attention I was accorded when I was a child," she says. "I am not really exposing my older child to the types of things I was exposed to because to some extent he's pulled down by his younger brother."

Even some only children who were happy growing up alone make starting a family a top priority. "There's one thing about being an only child," says Ruth Brine, a retired editor, "and that is your family dwindles down. After college, my family didn't exist except my mother and father. I decided I had to reconstitute a family. It made me want to have children, more than one child. I was interested, to an extent, in the man I married because he had two sisters, and there was a lot of family life that sort of fascinated me. Our Christmases when I was a little girl were very tiny—my father, mother, and grandparents. My father was a very fast eater. I don't think Christmas dinner lasted more than ten minutes. Then he'd go off to his club or ride horseback. Mother would disappear, and then I'd read. I wanted to have three children, which in fact I did."

An only child who is the last of her family has a particularly hard decision. "I'm the last of the Adler line," says Margot Adler, who is trying to decide whether or not to have a child. "I'm not into the genetic trip. But on the other hand, my family is a group of weird, interesting people. I have an aunt who's eighty-two, who was one of the first neurologists in Vienna, and she's still practicing as a shrink.

Her sister joined the Russian Revolution and later died in a
Stalinist concentration camp. It was a pretty heavy-duty
family, and here I am, the last of it all. I must admit I have
some kind of compunction to have a child partly for that
reason. And I also hate options closing. There's something
to having kids that ties you deeply to the human race."

There is a sizable contingent of only children, pretty
satisfied with life, who see procreation as problematic. Statistically, only children often come from homes that have
been split up by death or divorce. As a result, they may have
more trouble envisioning themselves as parents than people
who grew up in traditional nuclear families. As in other
areas of life, it helps to have a role model. Judy Anderson-
Wright, who grew up with her grandparents after her
mother's disappearance, admits: "I don't have the typical
family life to follow. My grandmother did grandmotherly
things, but she wasn't a mother. I've questioned, because of
the biological clock, my decision to remain childless. I think
the problem is just not ever having seen a woman in the
mother role."

There are also only children who feel that a husband is
company, a child is a crowd. Petra Clayton, the California
insurance representative, discusses why she feels reluctant
to become a mother. "Getting married was to me a big adjustment," she says. "I thought that's all I can handle, one
other person. To let in another one, a child, was just too
much. Just to live together with somebody, even a person
you love, means you can't do what you want to do. To live
together with one's parents is one thing because they set the
rules and you play by them. But to live with a peer where
you're both equal, you have to find a balance. When I got
married I wasn't getting married to be a mother."

Some only children who had happy and stable childhoods

feel just plain uncomfortable about having children. They feel that they lack the proper training or experience. I, like many other only children, had no young cousins to care for. My single baby-sitting experience lasted one hour and consisted mainly of making sure the baby didn't die while her mother was off on an emergency errand. As one only child puts it: "I'm the worst person to leave with a person who dribbles."

As far as babies are concerned, familiarity may breed comfort rather than contempt. Mary Catherine Bateson says that her mother, Margaret Mead, took photographs and movies of her as a baby and child. "Margaret was concerned that not having younger siblings—and correctly concerned—that I might not know about children. I did very little baby-sitting. When I was about to have my daughter, Vanni, she made copies of all the movies made during my childhood to show me, so that I could look at a baby."

Because girls who are only children tend to be brought up with male and female expectations, they may not be as quick to imagine themselves as mothers as girls raised more traditionally. "I remember when I was growing up that you would always think of what you'd be doing, what your life was going to be like," says Katherine Feinstein. "I never once ever thought of myself as having kids. In all my great fantasies, a child was never involved, which is terrible. I can honestly say the issue in my life is whether to have one child or none. The issue is not whether to have two or three. My husband is one of three. He thinks kids are the greatest thing in the world. He doesn't think you should have as many as you can, but he does think that you should have two. I, on the other hand, think you should have one or none."

Child rearing and achievement, particularly for women, are hard to combine. One successful only child now in her fifties, who never married, maintains: "I have no regrets about not having children. I never wanted to be a teacher or a nurse, for instance. My mother says I never played with baby dolls or played mother. She says I always preferred to read a book. I never wanted to be a person who did what everyone else wanted to do. I never had strong maternal instincts. And I think it's just as well that those people don't have children. If I'm a perfectionist and a demanding person, that would be an awful burden on a child."

Of course, it is possible to combine child rearing and career. One of the first women editors at *Time* magazine, Ruth Brine was always a high achiever: valedictorian of her high school class and Phi Beta Kappa at Vassar. "After I came to *Time,*" she says, "I wasn't so achievement-oriented because I always saw it as secondary to having a family. I had no family. I felt that was the most important thing to do, for me, not for everybody." Since retiring, Brine has been working on an anthology of articles from the Vassar alumnae magazine. "The question that comes up over and over with women of high achievement and careers is how can they manage to have a family and should they," says Brine. "It's a question that's not going to go away. Can you have both? The women's movement doesn't settle anything. It opened doors, but it doesn't help you with that basic decision. I thought then, and I still think now, it's an either/or proposition of career first or children first. You can do both, but one has to be your priority. I was lucky that my career was able to blossom after the children were grown."

What kind of parents do only children make? According to the study done by Sharryl Hawke and David Knox, 61 percent of the only children they interviewed believed that growing up without siblings affected the way they brought up their own children. Some of the effects were positive: allowing children more independence, spending more time with them, and valuing children more. The negative ranged from an aversion to sibling bickering to having a hard time putting the children first.

Writer Frederick Golden has two grown children. "You do sacrifice by having children," he says. "I guess it probably doesn't make any difference if you have three or four or five. But it probably makes a difference whether you have one or two. Once you get to a certain stage you get liberated. I like kids, but I find my patience runs out on them. I never encouraged my wife to have more children, although I certainly enjoyed having my kids. Especially the first. I was much more attentive to the first. The second one, I guess, got short shrift."

True Hall, an only child and realtor in Tenants Harbor, Maine, worries about being fair to each one of his six children. "I never really thought much about being an only child growing up," says Hall. "It bothered me more after I had the six children to think that I probably had advantages that they wouldn't have. I feel bad in a way that I was married so young. I often think I could have been a little more help if I'd been a little older and wiser perhaps."

Now in his fifties, Hall realizes that as an only child, he will eventually inherit his parents' entire estate. It will be harder for him and his wife to divide their worldly goods, since they own a couple of homes and some beautiful parcels of land on the ocean. "How do you divide things equally?" he asks. "The only way you possibly do it is if everything is liquid. We have properties that are sort of unique, and if they were ever sold, you could never get them back. So it's a real concern that all will be treated equally."

Sibling bickering seems to be one of the hardest things for

an only child to handle as a parent. It is a theme that comes up often. "I keep a lot inside and have a difficult time, sometimes, dealing with my five children who sometimes I don't think are as grateful as they should be," says Roger Staubach. "If I had grown up in a bigger family, I might have been more understanding."

Barbara Polk, who has two daughters and a son, had idealized what a family would be like. "Sometimes it's been hard for me to understand their fights," she says. "When they fought, I was just crushed. I love them all so much. I guess I probably never had a fight with anyone until I was married, because you don't fight with your friends. I couldn't imagine why they'd want to fight with one another. Then at night, they'd be up in bed talking together. I'd realize that it wasn't anything."

Clem and Dorothy, who live in Michigan, are two only children who had romantic notions of what it would be like to raise children. Dorothy remembers that even back when she was dating men, she would write down names for future children. After getting married, Dorothy and Clem stopped at four only because "Clem said we couldn't afford any more."

They were concerned at first that because they were two only children that their kids would miss the network of aunts, uncles, and cousins that most people have. When their eldest son was born, one of Clem's business associates came over to the house to see him. Dorothy remembers saying: "The poor little guy, he's never going to have cousins. He doesn't have any aunts and uncles." The man turned to her and said: "He's the lucky one. He'll choose them. He's not going to be stuck with them."

For Clem and Dorothy, their family lived up to their high expectations. They have fond memories of Sunday morn-

ings in bed, listening to the "pitter patter of little feet."
Dorothy remembers: "It was just joyous. We'd listen to all
the fun they were having and think about how we hadn't
had that. We were always thinking of all the stuff we
missed." The couple took household harmony as far as they
could: They never fought in front of the children. Dorothy
remembers: "If Clem came home and something was wrong,
I'd rush him out the back door and I'd say, 'Oh, who is this?
This isn't Clem.' He'd pick it up and walk right back in and
give everybody a big hello. The children all thought this was
a joke. After dinner when they were all studying, we could
go upstairs and discuss whatever was wrong rather than
wrecking dinner."

They are proud of the job they did in raising their children. "People would tell us that we were a special family
because we were always together and happy," says Clem.
"We thought every family was like ours until we found out
that everybody fights with each other."

Do only children do anything differently when they raise
children? Like the Michigan couple, they may try extra hard
for family harmony. Some work hard to make sure there are
plenty of friends. Like other people, only children may try
to avoid some of the pitfalls of their own childhoods.

Laura Stein-Stapleford, who has two children, makes sure
that they are not put on a pedestal the way she was. But she
has nothing against precocity. "Basically, Fred and I talk
about our days and let the children into the conversation if
they want to talk about our day," she says. "We bring them
up to it. Somewhere along the line, something's been rub-
bing off. John has great language for a four-year-old. In a
store one time, I wouldn't let him get something and he said,
'Mother, I think that's an arbitrary decision that we should
negotiate.' And I said, 'I hope this is an aberration.' And the
saleslady said, 'No wonder he talks like that, if you talk to

him like that.' I think that even though we have two now, I still have not lowered my vocabulary."

Marni Weil, who has just one son, says that she is trying to include Frederick in adult discussions without allowing him to be the center of attention. "The way I've brought him up is that he's part of the group," she explains. "If there are four of us, he's entitled to one quarter of the attention. I don't believe in seen and not heard, nor do I believe in monopoly."

Toni Falbo, an expert on only children who is one and has one, says that she tries to avoid overprotecting. "You have to make sure that you don't overdo for the kid, never let them get a hard knock," she maintains. "It's hard to see a child suffer, but they have to make their own way. Only children may grow up a little naïve. But how do you teach a child to be devious? Anyway, you'd be the target. A lot of only children get connived, but there are other gullible folks out there, too."

My unscientific observation is that only children seem to run in families. Hereditary infertility could be a factor. So could the fact that only children tend to marry later. Or it could simply be that only children, like other people, want to replicate the type of family in which they were raised. For many only children, the ideal family size may actually be three.

Robin Bruna, a retired teacher married to another only child, was adamant about stopping at one. "When I had my child, I made Joe promise I wouldn't have to do it again," says Robin. "I don't have any regrets, despite the fact that we won't have grandchildren. [Their daughter is unable to have children.] I notice that the fewer children people have, the closer they are. Those with one do more things together. They don't have as much to quarrel over. The more kids people have, the farther husband and wife seem to be apart.

After the children are gone, they don't know what to do together or say to each other. They gradually have to find out that the other one exists."

Most only children find great satisfaction in their off-spring. "My daughter is the most significant connection in my life," says Renée Franklin, the New York attorney. "I'm surprised each day by how deep it is. I still have some sense of wonder that I did this and I have this. The blood connection is so deep. Even with a close marriage, marriages break down. I've seen aunts and uncles more since the birth of my daughter. Suddenly you have children in common."

Having a baby can make an only child feel more connected to whatever family still exists. Meteorologist Flip Spiceland observes: "The little one has really brought us all a lot closer together. We're a lot closer now than we were in years past. My dad took an early retirement just so that they can continue to drive back and forth between St. Louis and Atlanta."

Only children do not necessarily become as doting as their own parents. Ruth Brine delights in her children and grand-children. But she is happy for the peace and quiet at home. "Most people worry about the empty nest," she chuckles. "I find it quite restful. I'm back to being an only child now, with a husband who treats me as the only one."

TALE OF A MARRIAGE
Mary Kay Shaw, college administrator, and Jim Shaw, university professor, two only children married to each other for thirty years, Amherst, Massachusetts:

Mary Kay: We grew up in the same small town in Ohio. We didn't know each other until high school. We were in the same high school marching band. I played clarinet, and the band director said he thought I should play oboe. My father said he'd call Rod Shaw, who was the best musician in the area. I was a sophomore in high school, and I began taking lessons from Jim's father.

Jim: All my life I was upstairs trying to do my homework with snare drummers and saxophonists, and I never heard it. But someone trying to play the oboe—that I heard. It's the worst sound on the face of the earth. So I went downstairs to see what was going on. My line has always been: She looked better than she sounded.

Mary Kay: I think I grew up feeling a little cheated that I was an only child.

Jim: And I felt fortunate. How's that for openers?

Mary Kay: I was an only child through default. My parents lost two other children.

Jim: My guess is that I was an only child because of financial reasons. After I was born, my father lost his job and was in the wrong job for ten years until they survived the Depression. I don't think it was me. It wasn't that they took one look at me and said never again. We were Depression kids, so I never felt like an anomaly being an only child.

Mary Kay: I think I felt a responsibility to be very good at whatever I was taking on. I don't know who puts those pressures on children, or how they're communicated, but it was very important to me. There were times when my parents would say it's okay to get a B. I was very competitive at sports: basketball, volleyball, swimming, Ping-Pong. On the honeymoon, I didn't know whether to beat him at Ping-Pong. First crisis, new bride. Remember this was thirty years ago. Do you let him win? Never.

Jim: I've never figured out whether I'm competitive or not. I gave up playing cards because I hated to lose. I don't think of myself as being overtly competitive. I was never conscious of trying to beat anyone.

Mary Kay: Why do you think you were first in the class?

Jim: I would think that only children tend to be achievers because of parental influence. But one reason could be that there's a spectrum from self-sufficiency to selfishness.

Mary Kay: I always wanted to have more than one child. We have three children whom I'd describe as very close. They all live in the Washington, D.C. area. They have carved out different lives, but they have overlapping circles. They rely on and enjoy each other. We work very hard to have times together.

Jim: When it came to raising three children, we lacked the experience. We've always said that we don't quite know what they're plotting. That sounds like a Cosby line. But there was a certain lack of insight. What is that relationship that they have? Are things really bad because they're fighting? They shouldn't fight, right? Or maybe they should be fighting more.

Mary Kay: Our son who has just graduated from college asked me just last summer if his dad and I had ever had an argument. I was just stunned. I said, you've got to be kidding! He said that they had been talking among the three of them and had commented that they had never heard us argue or disagree. And that was a conscious decision on our part that we would have a united front. To our children, we always looked like The Parents.

Jim: This is something we nurtured very carefully. We said: You guys be friends and fight us. Do not fight each other. She and I will be friends and fight you, and the three of you be friends, 'cause you're going to have each other, not us. We really kept it a generational argument.

Mary Kay: I worked in college admissions, so as they were getting ready to go off to school, the director of admissions offered to give a practice interview. Rhod came to interview with her. Afterward, she was laughing because Rhod kept referring to us as The Parents. It was very revealing. What I see children do is pit mother against dad or daddy against mother. I think all three of ours would say it was The Parents. So we were sort of allies. We'd disagree, sometimes vehemently, but never in their earshot.

Jim: I've always thought of us as being complementary, not similar. I don't think too much about the similarities. Maybe the reason we're in agreement so much is that there are so many unstated assumptions that we share, and they're so fundamental that they're not stated. Maybe we're not complementary but we're similar in some psychic way.

nine

AS
TIME
GOES
BY

_I_t seems that for the past ten or fifteen years, I've been rushing home with increasing frequency because of family illness. My father, stepmother, aunt, and uncle are all in their late seventies now. There have been heart attacks, operations, amputation, and spells in intensive care. When I lived in New York City, Boston was just a shuttle flight away. Now that I live on the West Coast, I must sit for six hours imagining the worst as I speed home. I have been girding myself for the catastrophic and inevitable. Losing parents is a universal ordeal. For me, it is particularly hard because I have no one with whom I can share it.

Every time I go home now, I try to ask as many questions as I can about my family and myself. I want to gather facts. Sometimes I feel like an archeologist. The last Christmas that my aunt was well enough to reminisce, I pressed her hard about what my mother had really been like. Did she have a good sense of humor? Yes. Was she independent? Well, women *weren't very independent back then. Did she have a sense of adventure? Well, no, there wasn't much opportunity. The answers were perfunctory.*

The next morning at breakfast, though, my aunt said that she had given some more thought to my question and remembered that my mother had taken flying lessons in the late nineteen-forties. I found this nugget of information thrilling, both because of what it told me about my mother and because it had been almost lost forever.

I tried to make the same kind of probe about my own past, but I was less successful. *Was I a nervous little girl? Oh, once in a while. Did I have a bad temper? Oh, no, you behaved perfectly.* It's harder to get people to tell you to your face what they thought of you.

When I began to write this book, I depended heavily on pictures of my childhood. I don't have a peer who shared my home or went with me on family vacations. Without those faded pictures, I would be at a loss to reconstruct my childhood. I would remember it only in broad strokes and a few little details. I could quiz my cousins Beth and Tim, but we spent only special events like Thanksgivings and Christmases together. If my house caught on fire, the first thing I would rescue, after my dog, would be my photo albums.

Since my teenage years, I have been consciously trying to share experiences with people I like. I take my friendships very seriously. In some ways, they are better than family relationships because they are more of a reflection of who I am and what I have freely chosen. But they don't go back quite far enough. I have one good friend with whom I can relive high school days and our skirmishes over controlling the school newspaper. I stay in touch with college friends who shared a picnic at Quabbin Reservoir or remember the time we wore hard hats in the newspaper office because of the falling plaster. There are the running friends, men and women I ran miles and miles with, raced with, trained with, people who saw me at my best and my worst. And when I got married, I was preceded down the aisle by two of my best friends, both only children, who are friends and surrogate sisters.

Perhaps I spend more time than average in writing letters, making

phone calls, checking up to find out where friends are and what they are
doing. I consider them an integral part of my life. When I lose touch with
an old friend, I feel that I have lost a facet of myself. As the years go by,
I hope my friends will be there with me, at least in spirit, remembering
the good times and bad, reaffirming my life and theirs.

When Betty Rollin's mother, Ida, was dying, at age seventy-six, of ovarian cancer, Rollin was at her side. She was
there for the hospitalization and the chemotherapy, for the
nausea and the pain. As Rollin wrote in her book *Last Wish,*
Ida told her: "I expected a death sentence. I didn't expect
torture." As the disease got more debilitating, Ida kept telling Betty that she wanted her life to end. Ida's plea became
more insistent as her life became more insufferable, and
Betty finally agreed to help her mother commit suicide.

As she researched lethal dosages of drugs, a subject taboo
with doctors, Rollin was afraid that she could be committing
a crime. But she was more afraid of ignoring her mother's
last wish. Once she had helped her mother collect the necessary drugs, Betty and her husband joined Ida for one last
family gathering. They spent some time looking over old
photo albums, and Ida told her daughter that she was the
happiest woman in the world. Ida committed suicide with
her daughter and son-in-law at her side. It was a dramatic
end to an intense relationship.

Few only children are faced with the harrowing choice
Betty Rollin had to make. But many find that they become
a lifeline and protector for aging parents. Watching the decline and death of a parent is one of life's worst experiences.
Only children must go through this crisis more or less alone.

Because only children tend to have older parents to begin
with, they often must deal with mortality sooner. The pros-

pect of providing for parents is something that some only children begin thinking about relatively early in life. Betty Ann Byerly, who is still in her twenties, is already worrying about how she will care for her parents. "The thought of losing my mom and dad brings tears to my eyes," she says. "As they get older, I want to take care of them, make them comfortable. I have a certain idea of how it should be handled. I can't see my parents in a rest home. My mother took care of her mother."

The years of decline can be a trying time for an only son or daughter. One man, who is in his forties, describes the difficulties with his parents, who are in their eighties: "They're both relying on me more and more to help them with practical judgments. It's harder for them to think through the things they want to do. I find myself having to make arrangements for them to do things: paying doctor bills, just the minutiae of life that should just take about five minutes to do. My mother will drag me aside and tell me how terrible my father is and all these things he's doing to make her life miserable. He will drag me aside and tell me the same things about her. They've been married for almost fifty years, but part of the vitality of their marriage is that they bicker with one another. Now I'm drawn into that.

"They don't have any estate, but they have a house and a little bit of savings. It's all coming to me. They keep saying this. It's wonderful, but I have sole responsibility for them in their old age, unless they go into a nursing home. And I sometimes think if there were two or three children, this particular cycle of family life would be much easier to manage. On the other hand, it might not be. Terrible fights between children get sparked off just at this moment. Who's going to get what? I know my own grandmother was shunted around from one to the next, and by the time she died all of her children hated one another."

Most only children feel a strong sense of obligation to care for their parents. Sometimes it comes from genuine devotion. Sometimes it is a continuation of a lifetime of parental expectations. Most of the time, it is a combination of both. Patricia Bresee, a commissioner of the Superior Court of San Mateo County, California finds "agony" in the role reversal. After her father retired, her parents sold their home and moved to California to be near her. After her father died, Bresee found that her mother became very demanding. Says Bresee: "Something hit me several months ago when she said 'I really envy my friend Ellen because her sons call her every night.' I thought, 'Let's face it, it's never going to work. I'm never going to make this lady happy.' I asked her, 'What do you want from me?' She said, 'I just want you to continue being my best friend.' I said, 'I don't want to be your best friend. I want to be your daughter.' "

Bresee wishes that she would end up with different memories of her parents. "It is already very, very hard to remember what must have been very good times," she says. "Mostly I remember how much I adored my father. But right now I feel a lot of anger toward my mother."

Especially if one parent has died, there can be a dependency that many only children find particularly troublesome. Kathy Gay, the IBM salesperson who spoke earlier about the problems of being forced to be an adult before her time, finds that she once again must fill a role for which she's not ready. Although she has just turned thirty, she finds herself supporting her mother. "My mother is very much convinced that since I'm the only child, and since she's been a widow for ten years—even though she's only sixty—that I should be supporting her even now," complains Gay. "Because I have done well and I'm all that she has, she thinks that I should be supporting her to at least the style that I'm living in. She feels that she shouldn't be working, that either she should be living with me or I should be sending her at least as much money as I keep for myself. I've often wished that there were a brother or sister to at least debate that idea with her. It's a lot of pressure."

"It's more common for only children to have older-than-average parents," observes psychologist Toni Falbo, herself an only child. "So that means that as only children become middle-aged, they're more likely to be losing their parents. But the burden of the only child is probably not as bad as one might guess. People who have one child may be more financially secure, so when they grow older, they may have more of a cushion to fall back on." She has also observed that even in large families, one child will get a disproportionate amount of work. "If you live closer to your aging parents, you're more likely to have to do the nitty-gritty of caring for them. My parents moved to live near where I am, and I think it's really terrific that I don't have to discuss the issues with somebody else. I don't need to do any negotiating. I know I'm in charge. I find that to be a tremendous comfort."

When an only child loses parents, he loses a great deal of his past. Gone is the family home, the older generation, and the remembrance of things past. In their book, *The Sibling Bond,* psychologists Stephen P. Bank and Michael D. Kahn observe: "Even though by adulthood most siblings have gradually separated and gone their different ways, the knowledge of each other's core identity remains as a legacy and a reminder of one's childhood past, submerged unverbalized, and only partially forgotten. To meet one's brother

or sister, even after many years, is to recapture the bitter-
sweet memory of one's own essential childhood self . . .
One's core self, seen through the eyes of a sibling, or compared with that of a sibling, remains as one essential reference point for personal identity." The only child does not
have that.

"The only time that I wished for a brother or sister was
when I was in my thirties," says Dick Cavett. "I thought it
would have been pleasant to have had someone else to
match impressions of my parents with, someone to compare
notes about growing up. I hear brothers and sisters jog each
others' memories. And you have another impression of your
parents from someone else. As I turned forty, I became more
aware of mortality—although like Woody Allen, I've always
been aware of it. I think it was then that I suddenly took an
interest in what had become of my high school friends. At
that time I thought: Dammit, if I only had a brother or sister
to check some of these facts with. What did we do that
summer? In later years, I thought there could be advantages
in having a brother or sister."

Laura Stein-Stapleford says she gets jealous of people
who have family reunions. "I really can't reune with anybody," she moans. "I am thirty-five and my mother could
live to be one hundred. But when my mother dies, my only
tie to my childhood is my friend Max, and that just goes
back to age fourteen. Sometimes I think that's downright
sad, but it's the best I can do, because my husband didn't
know me until I was twenty-four or twenty-five years old.
I criticize these people who went to grade school together,
who are all friends and have their little clique and are not
interested in meeting new people. I do think it's tunnel
vision. But I think it's nice that they have that sense of 'I
knew him when.' "

Marjorie Irwin, a retired schoolteacher, has cultivated and maintained lifetime connections. "I think I have a lot of friends that I have kept over the years," she says. "Most of my friends are ones that I made either in grade school or in high school and college. I tend to reach out to cousins. I have two cousins I'm close to. I need them for my generation now, for my childhood, for remembering. As long as Mother was living, there was someone to remember with. But now I find myself seeking these friends and seeking my cousins to remember with because there's nobody else around. Maybe it's because of my age. I had my fiftieth high school reunion, and that was good because I had someone to remember with."

Mary Catherine Bateson says that her mother, Margaret Mead, believed in the importance of photographs in evoking childhood, especially when there are no brothers or sisters. She, herself, has consciously done certain things so that her daughter, Vanni, will have that important connection to her past. "There are things you can do to protect a child from loss of memory," says Bateson. "Arranging for other playmates is important. You've got to have aunts and uncles, too. Forget biology. I feel strongly that there are going to be a lot of people who are not going to want to have children. One of the ways to have a humane society is to be sure that all adults have some relationship with some children. A lot of that has to be the initiative of the parents, because a lot of people don't have that model available of relating to children who are non-kin. You start inviting your unmarried friends over to dinner and establish some kind of honorary kinship." Bateson, herself, grew up living with surrogate families when her mother was off on field expeditions.

Bateson believes that only children—and everyone else, for that matter—would be better off if they had more flexible ideas about what constitutes family. "I've come to realize how much my mother's ideas about organized family life were derived from Samoa," she says. "Not so much on the issues of permissiveness, sexuality, or adolescence, but on the notion of families having flexible boundaries. One of the things she talks about in *Coming of Age in Samoa* is that if a family doesn't have a child, some relatives provide them with a child. If a child is quarreling with his parents, he can move to another household. Contrast that to the way people were locked into nuclear family households during the fifties. Once one says that it's better for children not to be locked into the nuclear family, you realize that society has a massive unmet need for uncles and aunts."

Annie Edwards, who had her only child when she was still a teenager, has consciously provided surrogate siblings for her daughter, Shauna. "If you leave yourself a little flexible in the world, you can be spontaneous," Edwards maintains. "You make a really good connection with a family of parents and kids and it clicks. Rather than letting it go and being lazy about it, there's a sort of a cultivation process where you let them know as much as you can that you love them and enjoy being with them." And Edwards encourages other kids to come live with the two of them. "It's really been kind of a chaotic scene as far as people going in and out. But it's like a heartbeat, an organic thing. It seems very vital and durable to me for that reason."

There is no question that only children put a very high value on friendship. These are not superficial relationships. They are deeply felt bonds, connections that in many ways resemble familial ties. An only child may need these friendships more than people with siblings. Close friendships are the only child's insurance against isolation.

Psychotherapist and author Lillian B. Rubin believes that for many people, friendship is "the neglected relationship." In her book, *Just Friends,* she writes: "The idea of kin is so deeply and powerfully rooted within us that it is the most common metaphor for describing closeness." In her study of friendship, however, she found that on many levels friendships are more important than kinships. While many people are stuck in rigid relationships with family members—relationships that seldom acknowledge the growth of the individual—they find themselves reflected more as they are in their friendships. People make friends because of common goals, interests, and experiences. Friends are a reflection of who we are at a given point in our lives. At their best, they can provide a lifetime of continuity and caring. As Sherri Elliott puts it: "I don't have sisters I can call up when I get into a jam. My friends are really, really important, and I make sure I take out the time to be with them. It's like being covered, I guess."

Elizabeth Topham Kennan, an only child who is a medieval scholar and the president of Mount Holyoke College, has taken a special interest in the idea of friendship, in part because of her studies of monastic life. Her own experiences have underscored the importance of friendship. An only child, she found herself widowed, the mother of a seriously handicapped son, over fifteen years ago. Friends were vital then. Now, despite the pressing duties of being the president of a small liberal arts college, Kennan continues to make friendship an enduring priority.

"I can remember vividly from the time I was two, maybe three, how important my friend from across the street was," recalls Kennan. "After I started school, I made friends with another only child, a girl. We were extremely close, playing together almost daily and moving in and out of each other's homes. The fact that you had to be friends with somebody who owed you no affection meant that you had to be more malleable."

Kennan learned one of the most important lessons about friendship when she moved into a new neighborhood. "I had a new set of friends," she remembers. "One of them came to the house and wanted me to do something. I told her that I didn't feel like doing that. My father overheard me and came to me, not quite angry, and said: 'What you don't realize is that friendship demands that you do what your friends want to do whether you want to or not.' I had never before seen him so exasperated with me. It had an enormous effect. Of course, I went right off and did what that friend wanted to do. It's been one of the most lasting memories of my life—and it still guides my thoughts about relationships with my friends or the people I care about."

Only children seem to long for close friendships more than people with siblings. "Perhaps there's a desire on the part of only children to project friendships backward," muses Kennan, "to create a past that never existed by pretending or allowing friendships to converge to pretended family relationships. I have one of them. When I was a teenager, I was friends with a girl five years younger. Our families were close friends. She came to college at Mount Holyoke because I had come to Mount Holyoke. She's still one of my very closest friends, and I always introduce her as my foster sister. It's a label that I've made up. But I think upon reflection, it's a way of engulfing the past."

Carmelita Thomson, a psychotherapist in her early fifties, observes: "I think we only children try to make sisters out of everybody. There may be a tendency to want, not necessarily more friends, but a more intimate relationship with those you do call friends. Maybe it's because only children are really good at one-on-one."

Only children frequently form their closest attachments to other only children. "Families impose a discipline from the time children are very young that they must help a brother or sister whether they want to or not," says Kennan. "If you help a member of the family, you can count on someone helping you in times of stress. Only children act that way with friends, but not all friends reciprocate. It's much more likely that the friends who are only children reciprocate. The friends who aren't are more likely to exhibit that generosity of spirit to siblings. It's that different form of acculturation."

In establishing friendships, only children sometimes adopt that long-lost brother or sister. "My friend Max, who is essentially an only child, is the closest thing I have to a brother," says Laura Stein-Stapleford. "When there are crises in our lives, we always turn to each other, even though we're happily married. The relationship now is what we both perceive it would be like to have a sibling. I think that only children tend to form the closest relationships with other only children because they are not in competition with their friends' siblings for attention and loyalty. We aren't distracted by the needs of our siblings. We tend to focus more attention on our friends. We don't feel that blood is necessarily thicker than water."

Carmelita Thomson believes that only children may ultimately have a special ability to connect with others. She observes: "I think only children may have the potential capacity to really value others in a way that it's never quite taken for granted. I think that's positive. My granddaughter has an intense longing to be with other kids, and I think that's because she's an only child. The implications of that may be the ability to really understand the significance of a relationship, of bonding with other people. And that's the primary way we are human."

At some point in life, only children, like everyone else, must take stock. Where are they going? Who will be with them? Even only children who have offspring of their own seem to feel a need for strong friendships. Thomson, who has been divorced for fifteen years, has four children. "Three of my kids are male, and I really like them and we can talk, but they're not here," she says. "Because they're your kids and not your friends, there's not the same reciprocity. There are times when it's really nourishing for me to see my kids, but I think of that as temporary. I don't really expect them to fulfill my needs."

An only child, especially one without children, must consider some unpleasant possibilities. Lynne Humkey, the only child of two only children, is still in her thirties. She is married, but cannot have children because of a medical condition. Humkey worries: "If something happens to my husband—either he dies or we get divorced—his family may love me, except in a divorce situation. But I don't care what anybody, even my husband, says. I'm not going to fit in as if I were a Humkey by birth. So that kind of bothers me. When my folks are gone, if something happens to Don, all I've got is his family. If his family is too busy with their own lives, which they very well might be, I'm pretty much on my own."

Distressing as this prospect might be, Humkey has a typical only-child solution. Like Kennan and Stein-Stapleford, she has formed enduring friendships with other only children. Together, they've discussed the unhappy prospect of being left completely alone. "If anything happens, we were joking we'd get our own place and have a little old ladies' retirement farm," chuckles Humkey. "It would be us and our horses. It's kind of funny, but it's not."

With the careful cultivation of friends and relations, an only child need not be alone in a time of crisis. When Elizabeth Kennan found herself widowed with a severely handicapped, five-year-old child, people came to her aid. "That was a time of very high anxiety," she says. "I turned to friends because I desperately needed them. I was met by such a wide-ranging network that it really expanded my capabilities and interests as a person."

Now in her late forties, she is remarried. Her aging parents live nearby. Her son is away at school. "I still find myself sometimes with a shadow of worrying about loneliness," she admits. "I've noticed in the past few years how much siblings enjoy one another. I enjoy my former husband's sister's family in a very active way, and I've been generously kept in that family." Like many other only children, Kennan is philosophical about life. "I find myself aware that there are some things I will never have and notice in passing that it would have been wonderful. But it's not an active sense of loss, just a recognition that life is never full for any individual."

A LIFE
Gail Roper, late fifties, swim coach and former Olympian, Menlo Park, California:

I thought about being an only child more when I was young, when I was in elementary school. My mother was divorced. People didn't talk about things like that back then. I felt like there was

something wrong with me. I used to be so naïve.
I'd tell people I just didn't have a father. People
would laugh at me. When I got older, I realized
you couldn't say that. But in a sense, I really believed I just had a mother. I was only six months
old when my parents got divorced.

I had aunts and uncles, a grandmother and
grandfather. We all lived in the same house. I was
the only young person in the house. They were
always telling me to go out and play. I started
swimming when I was two. We lived across the
street from a creek that was an offshoot from the
Delaware River. It was about six feet deep, thirty
yards across, with a strong current. It was called
the Waterpower, and fed waterpower into the
mills. Further on, there was a big hydroelectric
dam. You had to learn to swim, because as soon
as you'd jump in, you'd be swept along.

When I went to high school, there was a swimming team. Someone told the teacher that Gail
Peters could swim. I was so excited to be able to
swim. We wouldn't train more than an hour. And
we were allowed to swim only one lap at a time.
After I graduated, I still kept swimming. My
mother would say, "What do you want to do that
for?"

I knew I needed a coach, so one day I hitchhiked
to Rutgers University, where there was a well-
known swimming coach. I asked him if he would
coach me, and he asked me how much I could pay.
I told him I had hitchhiked there, and I had no
money. He said that he charged thirty-five dollars
a week, which was a lot of money, and that he

wouldn't coach anyone for free. I hitchhiked back
to Trenton, really dejected.

I started reading everything I could about swimming and the best swimmers. I learned what kind
of workouts they did and who they trained with.
I started winning at some meets. My mother became interested in the social aspects of it. She
never gave me any money, but she would drive me
to meets. She'd sit around with the other people
and talk. She liked being known as the mother of
Gail Peters. But she really didn't care about the
swimming.

I coached myself to third place in the nationals,
still training myself. When I got to the nationals
in Detroit, I was twenty-two. Jim Campbell, from
Walter Reed Hospital, was there. He was a very
dynamic, flamboyant, loudmouthed coach. When
Jim Campbell yelled, you could hear him all over
the pool. I decided that's what I wanted, a coach
who would really yell at me. My mother went
over and talked to him because I was so shy. He
said I could come down to Washington to talk to
him.

I took a Greyhound bus down to Washington,
D.C. He only wanted top swimmers, so anytime
anyone went to him, he'd give them this terrible
workout, wanting them to quit, trying to make
them or break them on that first day. I loved it. I
moved to Washington, got a job with the government as a draftsman for the Geological Survey,
and trained hard.

I was twenty-three when I was in the Olympics.
It was almost like a gimmick. I'm a success at

twenty-three or twenty-four. For the rest of my life, I don't have to do a thing. A lot of Olympians have trouble coming back, especially if they don't win a medal. But I set a world record the following year.

I got married when I was twenty-seven and started to have children. I had seven in all. Growing up, a lot of my friends were Catholic and had big families. It seemed more like the ideal home. I was doing what was expected, what was normal, what the Bible said, what was the accepted role. I believed that if you were a good wife, your husband would never leave; you'd never be alone. In my dream, happiness equaled a big family.

I was married seven years the first time. My husband was Japanese, and he didn't have the same values I did. I was married to my second husband for fourteen years. He was an achiever. We both wanted a big family. He was a real estate promoter and also an alcoholic. I was trying everything to make things work. Something seemed missing all the time. I had three kids in diapers at once. He never helped. He couldn't even turn on the washing machine.

Eventually, masters' swimming started. I hadn't swum at all for about twenty years. I dreamed of big swimming meets. I began setting age-group records. No one's ever set records in as many strokes as I have. I was good at distance and sprinting. I held all national records once in two age groups.

When I got divorced the second time, I was forty-nine years old. I had seven kids and no skills. I decided to go back to college at the University of Hawaii. I was terrified. I thought that when people got over thirty their brains stopped working. But when I took the entrance exam, I got the second highest mark.

I guess I reinvented myself. I discovered you don't have to be locked into anything. I became a marine biologist. I've always felt I was unique. I don't understand why. As an only child, I spent a lot of time by myself. It's a wonder that I didn't die, the way I wandered. I'd go into the woods and sit by myself. I had a lot of time to observe. That's why I'm in the field I'm in. I observe nature.

I was very lonely when I was married. I'm not lonely at all now. I lost my job with the Fish and Wildlife Department a year ago. Now I call myself a swimming coach. I coach men and women masters swimmers at Stanford. It would really be a strain for me to afford an apartment, so I live out of my truck. I have a storage room for my things. I have a phone line in there with an answering machine. And I housesit for people. And travel.

I'm in charge of my life now. I know what I like. I don't feel guilty about my swimming. I am worried about my degenerative arthritis. The doctor told me that I shouldn't swim anymore, and I walked out of his office determined to swim. Sometimes I can't get my arm out of the water. The pain is too much. I think, now what? Then I readjust the game plan. I stopped doing the backstroke and the breaststroke. Then the butterfly went out. I didn't swim for three months. It was hard to get up on the starting block again. I started losing some races. But I thought, what's worse: sitting at home and feeling bad or losing some races?

Sometimes I think: Whatever you've had, you've used it up. But I've started traveling. I went to China a year ago, and this year I'm going to South Africa. I started to lake swim. I hope a grant comes through so that I can get my job back with the Fish and Wildlife Department, if not here, then in Hawaii.

Once I found out that you don't have to live by the rules, life became much better. Now that I'm single, I don't have to consult anyone else. If people don't accept you, find new friends. I'm busy all the time. People say: You live in your truck? Having an apartment doesn't mean as much to me as being free and traveling. The people who sit at home, they're the lonely ones. I believe in taking a lot of chances.

My mother worried about what would happen to her. She put money away, bought a house. Her mind went, and she had to live in a rest home for four years. After four months, she used up her life savings. I felt bad. At the time, I was living in Hawaii on welfare with six kids. I couldn't help. It was a heartbreaking thing. But I had to put my children before my mother.

My eldest daughter thinks I'm pretty wonderful. She's thirty-two. Three of my other children think I have problems. Sarah, who's twenty-two, cares about me. Sabrina Sunshine is trying to find herself. My son, Jim, who's eighteen, thinks I'm great.

I don't know which one of them will come through if I need them. As you get older, you make better friends. You know who you are, and they get to be the people you rely on. I don't believe there is anyone else but me in charge of me. When you're alone, you learn that. I think I can give more now to other people without asking for anything back. I don't need anything back. Maybe that's part of being an only child. Life is good.

AFTERWORD

In the introduction, I mentioned that one's feelings about being an only child often change over time. A number of friends have asked me if, during the course of writing this book, I've had a change of heart, or if I have any new insights into being an only child.

I never meant this book to be about me or my perceptions. But as I was writing it, my editor urged me to make the book more personal. Like many another only child, I'm a rather private person. And as a journalist, I seldom write in the first person. Yet, my editor was correct. My own experiences did keep barging in and shaping the book. Eventually I got over some of my queasiness about writing about myself. In some ways, it was very therapeutic to recover the past. In other ways, it was very painful. Nobody particularly relishes looking back on an awkward adolescence.

But I do have a confession to make: For the first time in my life, I disliked being an only child. During the course of writing this book, my aunt, who raised me, hovered near death for seven months, dying by inches. Sometimes I felt I couldn't both write this book and be home when I was needed. I felt very much in need of a brother or sister—or someone—who could fill in for me. My aunt's impending death gave me a sense of urgency. She died just weeks after I finished the last chapter.

With her passing, certain negative aspects of being an only child were driven home. I know that much of my early life is lost forever, and that there are aspects of family history I will never know. My aunt's death also made me feel the need to try to reconstitute a family—not necessarily a family that is genetically related to me, but certainly a family that I can depend upon. And I did, for the first time, start to think about what life might be like if I were seventy years old and alone.

Another confession: One of the great curses of being an only child is the desire to be perfect. This flaw ran amuck during the course of writing this book. I had terrible recurring nightmares. I'd wake up in the middle of the night, anxious and afraid that I had forgotten to call a most important person. Or that I had promised something and forgotten. Sometimes I would dream that there were two women outside my house who were angry that I hadn't done something. That, of course, was a subconscious reference to my editor and agent, who, in fact, were extremely patient and encouraging.

I've come to the conclusion that as time goes by, the fundamentally positive facts about being an only child still apply. If I could alter the course of my own history, I would not go back and ask my mother and father to give me a sibling. Every life is made up of a mosaic of personal strengths and weaknesses, of infinite possibilities. I guess, like Betty Rollin, I'm one of those "it's for the best" people. I never considered myself disadvantaged. I never had to deal with poverty, alcoholism, violence, or many of the serious problems that afflict families. I didn't have a learning disability or a serious health problem. When I consider all the awful things that can happen to people, I think I've been extremely lucky.

Part of that luck, I'm convinced, comes from being an only child. When I began writing this book, I left my job of twelve years, my apartment of ten, my friends of forever, and moved to a new part of the country to begin a new stage of life. I was not alone, of course. But I was setting up my first household with my husband. It was a lot of change to endure, and sometimes I had my doubts about whether I could handle it. I can see now that my capacity to adapt to new circumstances is one of my greatest strengths. Many traits that I've taken for granted—self-reliance, sensitivity, flexibility—are directly attributable to the way I grew up. Despite new distances, friendships have increased, not diminished, in importance.

I hope I've presented a fair-minded assessment of what it's like to be an only child. I still believe that it is an advantage. Despite some of the unhappy experiences I had in the past year, I have no regrets about being an only child. I may try to be a perfectionist in certain areas of life, but I certainly don't expect life to be perfect.

ACKNOWLEDGMENTS

There are many people to thank and acknowledge for their help in creating this book. First of all, I'd like to express my gratitude to all the only children who let me enter their lives and share their experiences. Self-exploration is not always the most comfortable of pursuits, and these people did it selflessly.

My agent, Suzanne Gluck, believed in this book when many people did not think the subject was "marketable." She not only represented me well; she was available beyond the call of duty, helping to locate only children, reading the final manuscript with critical care, and encouraging me when I felt overwhelmed.

My editor, Maria Guarnaschelli, steered this book in the right direction. I never would have written about myself if she had not forced me to do so. Her instincts about this book were better than mine.

A number of people were instrumental in helping me finish this project. When I was at a serious impasse, Barbara Graham helped me recover my childhood in a way that I could finally write about it. She read the manuscript, offered important suggestions, and was always willing to put her own work aside to help me with mine. Every writer should have such a friend.

Denise Murphy gave me invaluable help with interviews, research, and transcription. She was clever and dependable, and I would have been completely swamped without her. Elizabeth Taylor gave the manuscript a thorough and professional read and bolstered my confidence. At various stages of the manuscript, I called upon Wendy Edelstein, Alison Merrilees, and Debby Wells for aid that was ably and quickly given out of both interest and friendship. Holly Mak and David Giveans also read the manuscript and helped with tone and accuracy. Toni Falbo, who probably knows more about only children than anyone else, was generous in providing information as well as encouragement.

Finally, I'd like to thank my family: Ed and Gladys, Mary and Jerry, for all their contributions; my husband, Paul Witteman, for his patience and input; and my dog, Scoop, for sitting next to me all those days while I slaved away at my computer. I could not have finished without their support.

—ELLIE MCGRATH
San Francisco

NOTES

CHAPTER ONE: THE MYTHOLOGY

19 *Gallup Report,* May 1986.

20 G. Stanley Hall, *Aspects of Childhood Life and Education,* ed. T. L. Smith (Boston: Ginn, 1907).

20 Toni Falbo and Denise F. Polit, *A Quantitative Review of the Only-Child Literature: Research Evidence and Theory Development,* Texas Population Research Center Papers, No. 7.006.

21 Judith Blake, "The Only Child in America: Prejudice Versus Performance," *Population and Development Review* 7, No. 1, March 1981.

21 Phyllis A. Katz and Sally L. Boswell, "Sex-Role Development and the One-Child Family," *The Single-Child Family,* ed. Toni Falbo (New York: Guilford Press, 1984), pp. 63–116.

22 Frances Hodgson Burnett, *The Secret Garden* (New York: J. B. Lippincott, 1911).

22 Kay Thompson, *Eloise: A Book for Precocious Grown-Ups* (New York: Simon & Schuster, 1955).

23 Benjamin Spock, *Baby and Child Care* (New York: Pocket Books, 1976); Benjamin Spock and Michael B. Rothenberg, *Dr. Spock's Baby and Child Care* (New York: Pocket Books, 1985).

23 John Leo, "Bringing Dr. Spock Up to Date," *Time,* April 8, 1985.

23 Murray Kappelman, *Raising the Only Child* (New York: Signet, 1975), p. 27.

23 Maya Pines, "Only Isn't Lonely (Or Spoiled Or Selfish)," *Psychology Today,* March 1981.

23 Norman M. Lobsenz, "Sometimes It's Good to Be an Only Child," *Parade,* February 23, 1986.

24 Bryce J. Christensen, " 'Only Child' Syndrome Is a Threat to American Society," *Chicago Sun-Times,* November 12, 1986.

24 Ben J. Wattenberg, *The Birth Dearth* (New York: Pharos Books, 1987).

25 Christopher Wren, "One Side Effect of Birth Control in China: The Brat," *The New York Times,* December 25, 1982.

26 Edward Goldwyn (producer), *Only Child in China,* a NOVA film, produced by the BBC, 1983.

26 Robert Pear, "Chinese Who Shun 1-Child Plan Get U.S. Asylum," *The New York Times,* August 6, 1988.

27 Landon Y. Jones, *Great Expectations* (New York: Ballantine Books, 1981).

28 Ellen Peck and Judith Senderowitz, eds., *Pronatalism: The Myth of Mom & Apple Pie* (New York: Thomas Y. Crowell Company, 1974).

30 H. Theodore Groat, Jerry W. Wicks, and Arthur G. Neal, "Without Siblings: The Consequences in Adult Life of Having Been an Only Child," *The Single-Child Family,* ed. Toni Falbo, pp. 253–89.

CHAPTER TWO: THE TIE THAT BINDS

37 Gloria Vanderbilt, *Once Upon a Time* (New York: Alfred A. Knopf, 1985).

38   Sharryl Hawke and David Knox, *One Child By Choice* (Engle-
      wood Cliffs, N.J.: Prentice-Hall, Inc., 1977).

40   Marilyn Fabe and Norma Wikler, *Up Against the Clock: Career
      Women Speak on the Choice to Have Children* (New York: Ran-
      dom House, 1979).

40   Barbra Walz and Jill Barber, *Starring Mothers* (New York:
      Dolphin Books, 1987).

41   James Schaffer and Colleen Todd, *Christian Wives: Women
      Behind Evangelists Reveal Their Faith in Modern Marriage* (Garden
      City, N.Y.: Doubleday, 1987).

41   Alice Walker, "One Child of One's Own: A Meaningful
      Digression Within the Work(s)," *In Search of Our Mothers'
      Gardens* (New York: Harcourt Brace Jovanovich, 1983).

43   Sharryl Hawke and David Knox, *One Child By Choice*,
      p. 79.

47   Erich Segal, *Love Story* (New York: Harper & Row, 1970),
      pp. 58, 62.

47   Dee Presley, Billy, Rick, and David Stanley, as told to
      Martin Torgoff, *Elvis: We Love You Tender* (New York: Dela-
      corte Press, 1979), pp. 7–8, 41.

48   Nicholas Von Hoffman, *Citizen Cohn* (New York: Double-
      day, 1988), p. 65.

51   Monica Morris, *Last Chance Children* (New York: Columbia
      University, 1988).

51   Adam Hochschild, *Half The Way Home: A Memoir of Father and
      Son* (New York: Viking, 1986) p. 3.

53   Barbara Kantrowitz, "Only But Not Lonely," *Newsweek*,
      June 16, 1986.

53   Denise Polit, "The Only Child in Single-Parent Families,"
      The Single-Child Family, ed. Toni Falbo, pp. 178–210.

55   Barbara Graham, *Jacob's Ladder* (New York: Dramatists' Play
      Service, Inc., 1987).

CHAPTER THREE: COMING FIRST: PRIVILEGED AND PRECOCIOUS

69   Elizabeth Whelan, *A Baby? . . . Maybe* (New York: Bobbs-
      Merrill, 1975).

71   Book Fredrick, *Hans Christian Andersen: A Biography* (University of Oklahoma Press, 1962).

73   Candice Feiring and Michael Lewis, "Only and First-Born Children: Differences in Social Behavior and Development," *The Single-Child Family,* ed. Toni Falbo, pp. 25–62.

73   Margo Howard, *Eppie: The Story of Ann Landers* (New York: G. P. Putnam's Sons, 1982), p. 65–66.

76   "The Real Romance," *Time,* February 26, 1951, p. 39.

76   Margaret Truman, *Bess W. Truman* (New York: Macmillan, 1986), pp. 366–67.

77   Lillian Belmont and Francis Marolla, "Birth Order, Family Size, and Intelligence," *Science,* 1973, p. 182.

78   Robert B. Zajonc, "Dumber By the Dozen," *Psychology Today,* January 1975.

79   John G. Claudy, "The Only Child As a Young Adult," *The Single-Child Family,* ed. Toni Falbo, p. 220.

81   Jean-Paul Sartre, *The Words* (New York: George Braziller, 1964), pp. 30, 144, 165.

CHAPTER FOUR: SIBLINGS AND SOCIAL SKILLS

94   Stephen P. Bank and Michael D. Kahn, *The Sibling Bond* (New York: Basic Books, 1982), p. 296.

97   Margo Howard, *Eppie,* p. 42.

100   John Updike, untitled essay on growing up in the 1940s, *Five Boyhoods,* ed. Martin Levin (New York: Doubleday & Company, 1962), p. 159.

102   John G. Claudy, W. S. Farrell, and C. Dayton, *The Consequences of Being an Only Child: An Analysis of Project TALENT Data, Final Report No. NO1-HD-82854* (Washington, D.C.: Center for Population Research, National Institutes of Health, December 1979), p. 32.

108   Sammy Davis, Jr., *Yes I Can* (New York: Farrar, Straus & Giroux, 1965), p. 33.

111   Kareem Abdul-Jabbar, *Giant Steps* (New York: Bantam Books, 1983).

CHAPTER FIVE: ALONE (BUT NOT NECESSARILY LONELY)

121   W. A. Swanberg, *Citizen Hearst* (New York: Charles Scribner's Sons, 1961).

122   Louise Bernikow, *Alone in America: The Search for Companionship* (New York: Harper & Row, 1986), p. 5.

126   Barbara Goldsmith, *Little Gloria . . . Happy At Last* (New York: Alfred A. Knopf, 1980), p. 437.

126   Gloria Vanderbilt, *Once Upon a Time* (New York: Alfred A. Knopf, 1985), p. 43.

128   Anthony Storr, *Solitude: A Return to the Self* (New York: The Free Press, Macmillan, 1988), pp. 17, 21.

CHAPTER SIX: INDEPENDENCE AND INDIVIDUALISM

145   Kenneth W. Terhune, *A Review of the Actual and Expected Consequences of Family Size* (Washington, D.C.: Government Printing Office, 1974).

146   Hawke and Knox, *One Child By Choice,* p. 26.

146   L. Frank Baum, *The Wonderful Wizard of Oz* (New York: Books of Wonder/William Morrow and Co., 1987).

150   Nathaniel Hawthorne, *The Scarlet Letter* (New York: Fred DeFau & Co., 1902), pp. 82, 168.

153   Phyllis A. Katz and Sally L. Boswell, "Sex-Role Development and the One-Child Family," *The Single-Child Family,* ed. Toni Falbo, pp. 63–116.

156   Bennett Simon, "The Hero as an Only Child," *International Journal of Psychoanalysis,* Vol. 55, 1974, pp. 555–62.

156   Anthony Storr, *Solitude: A Return to the Self,* p. 81.

158   F. Scott Fitzgerald, *The Great Gatsby* (New York: Charles Scribner's Sons, 1953), pp. 65, 99.

158   Lyn Tornabene, *Long Live the King: A Biography of Clark Gable* (New York: G. P. Putnam's Sons, 1976), p. 39.

159   Anthony Summers, *Goddess: The Secret Lives of Marilyn Monroe* (New York: Macmillan, 1985); Fred Guiles, *Norma Jean:*

The Life of Marilyn Monroe (New York: McGraw-Hill, 1969).

159   Brad Darrach, "The Triumph of Archie Leach," *People,* December 15, 1986.

CHAPTER SEVEN: SUCCESS AND THE SINGLE CHILD

171   Richard D. Lyons, "Each Astronaut Is an Only Child," *The New York Times,* December 21, 1968.
171   "Men of the Year: Astronauts Anders, Borman and Lovell," *Time,* January 3, 1969.
173   Walter Toman and Eleanore Toman, "Sibling Positions of a Sample of Distinguished Persons," *Perceptual and Motor Skills,* No. 31, 1970.
173   Lee Eisenberg and Lisa Grunwald, "A Census of America's New Leadership Class," *Esquire,* December 1985.
175   George Gallup, Jr., and Alec M. Gallup, with William Proctor, *The Great American Success Story* (Homewood, Illinois: Dow Jones-Irwin, 1986).

CHAPTER EIGHT: MERGING: MARRIAGE AND CHILDREN

192   Hawke and Knox, *One Child By Choice,* pp. 140–41.

CHAPTER NINE: AS TIME GOES BY

210   Betty Rollin, *Last Wish* (New York: Linden Press/Simon and Schuster, 1985), p. 91.
213   Bank and Kahn, *The Sibling Bond,* p. 60.
217   Lillian B. Rubin, *Just Friends: The Role of Friendship in Our Lives* (New York: Harper & Row, 1985), p. 16.

INDEX

ABOUT THE AUTHOR

Ellie McGrath was born in Gloucester, Massachusetts, and graduated magna cum laude from Mount Holyoke College. She has written for *Time* magazine for more than ten years, covering such diverse subjects as education, national politics, and the Olympics. She lives in San Francisco with her husband, Paul Witteman.